LESSONS IN REBELLION FROM THE PARABLES OF JESUS

subversive kingdom

Ed Stetzer

LifeWay Press®
Nashville, Tennessee

Published by LifeWay Press®
© 2011 Ed Stetzer

ISBN 978-1-4158-6977-2
Item 005371682

Dewey decimal classification: 231.72
Subject headings: KINGDOM OF GOD \ JESUS CHRIST--PARABLES \ CHURCH

This is a resource in the Christian Growth Study Plan. Visit *www.lifeway.com/cgsp* for more information.

All Scripture quotations are taken from the Holman Christian Standard Bible®, Copyright © 1999, 2000,
2002, 2003, 2009 by Holman Bible Publishers. Used by permission. Holman Christian Standard Bible®,
Holman CSB®, and HCSB® are federally registered trademarks of Holman Bible Publishers.

To order additional copies of this resource: write to LifeWay Church Resources
Customer Service; One LifeWay Plaza; Nashville, TN 37234-0113;
fax (615) 251-5933; phone toll free (800) 458-2772; order online at
www.lifeway.com; e-mail *orderentry@lifeway.com*; or visit the LifeWay Christian Store serving you.

Printed in the United States of America

Leadership and Adult Publishing
LifeWay Christian Resources
One LifeWay Plaza
Nashville, TN 37234-0175

subversive kingdom

About the Author

Ed Stetzer has planted, revitalized, and pastored churches. He has trained pastors and church planters on five continents, holds two masters degrees and two doctorates, and has written dozens of articles and books. Ed is a contributing editor for *Christianity Today*, a columnist for *Outreach Magazine* and *Catalyst Monthly*, serves on the advisory council of Sermon Central and Christianity Today's Building Church Leaders, and is frequently cited or interviewed in news outlets such as *USA Today* and CNN.

Ed Stetzer
President of LifeWay Research

Ed is Visiting Professor of Research and Missiology at Trinity Evangelical Divinity School, Visiting Research Professor at Southeastern Baptist Theological Seminary, and has taught at 15 other colleges and seminaries. He also serves on the Church Services Team at the International Mission Board.

Ed's primary role is the President of Lifeway Research.

He has written the following books:
- *Planting New Churches in a Postmodern Age* (2003)
- *Perimeters of Light: Biblical Boundaries for the Emerging Church* (with Elmer Towns, 2004)
- *Breaking the Missional Code* (with David Putman, 2006)
- *Planting Missional Churches* (2006)
- *Comeback Churches* (with Mike Dodson, 2007)
- *11 Innovations in the Local Church* (with Elmer Towns and Warren Bird, 2007)
- *Compelled by Love: The Most Excellent Way to Missional Living* (with Philip Nation, 2008)
- *Lost and Found* (with Richie Stanley and Jason Hayes, 2009)
- *Viral Churches* (with Warren Bird, 2010)
- *Spiritual Warfare & Missions* (with Jerry Rankin, 2010)
- *Transformational Church* (with Thom Rainer, 2010)
- *MissonShift* (with David J. Hesselgrave, 2010)

LEARNING TO REBEL

What kind of response would you get if you took a random survey of the world, asking them one simple question:

"What is a Christian?"

Perhaps several:

> "Christians are the people who go to church."
> "Christians are the people who believe in Jesus."
> "Christians are the people who don't have any fun."

It's all about perspective, isn't it? But here is one answer that isn't likely to make the list:

"Christians are the rebels."

In terms of the kingdom of God, that's exactly what we are. But to see the true rebel nature of Christianity, you have to understand a bit about the kingdom of God. God was, is, and always will be the rightful and sovereign Ruler of the universe. But humanity, because of our nature and choices, has cast off His rule in mutiny and chosen to live as rebels to His kingdom.

But when we became Christians, we entered into the kingdom of God, though the rest of the world is still in rebellion. Now, in a sense, we are the new rebellion ... the rebellion against the rebellion.

But what is life like in this counter rebellion? How are we to live as the rebels in the subversive kingdom? How do we remain faithful to our true King in a hostile environment? These are imperative questions for us if we truly want to embrace the kingdom of God.

This is a study of the parables Jesus told in the Book of Matthew to illustrate life in this kingdom. By studying these parables, you and your Bible study group will learn how radically different and rebellious life is in the *Subversive Kingdom*. Over the next six sessions, you will spend time reading, thinking through, and discussing the kingdom of God and what it means to be an agent of it.

HERE'S HOW IT WORKS:

This study includes opportunities for both individual and group study. Engaging in the individual daily devotions then participating in a Bible study group, which includes video teaching and discussion, is the best way to gain the fullest understanding of these lessons in rebellion.

At the beginning of each session, you will find the guide for the Bible study group portion of the study. Each meeting should follow this general outline:

Getting Started: Each week will begin with a time of discussion that helps you and your group get to know each other better and discuss what the Lord has been teaching you over the previous week. This part of the group will also help introduce the video teaching and the individual study for the coming week (15 min.).

Pressing In: Your group will watch a 10–15 minute teaching segment from the DVD while filling in the listening guide provided. Then, after the teaching segment, your group will discuss the ideas you've seen presented using the questions provided in the group experience. Close with prayer (35 min.).

Launching Out: The group experience each week wraps up with a key verse of Scripture to memorize and some specific challenges to engage in as you seek to live as a rebel in the *Subversive Kingdom*.

The teaching segment and discussion will propel you forward, as an individual, into your study throughout the week. You'll notice that after the group experience each week, there is another parable, one written for this book, that will hopefully help you understand more and more the idea of the kingdom of God. Like all parables, you can't interpret this one completely literally; it's merely a tool to help you see the big principles of the kingdom of God.

You'll continue looking at the Scriptures and ideas presented in your group by completing the five personal devotions. The next week, you'll come back to your group ready to begin another discussion based on the individual work you've done.

Throughout these six sessions, you will be greatly challenged and encouraged by these verbal pictures of life in the kingdom of God. I pray you will gain an even deeper love and appreciation for the true king and just how subversive His reign is. I hope you'll catch a vision and determine to be part of the rebellion against the rebellion—to be a rebel fully given over to the *Subversive Kingdom*.

subversive
kingdom

kingdom perspective

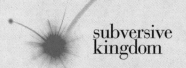
subversive
kingdom

SESSION 1

GETTING STARTED

1. Introduce yourself, and share one personal fact that will help your group get to know you better.

2. Share what you hope to gain from this study.

3. How important do you think it is to have an understanding of the kingdom of God? Why?

4. As a group, list words that come to mind when you hear the phrase, "kingdom of God."

PRESSING IN

Watch the teaching segment from the DVD using the viewer guide below.

The kingdom of God comes _____ in the perfect Son of God.

Jesus mentions the kingdom of God over _____ _____ in the Synoptic Gospels.

Jesus came to _____ the lost and to _____ the hurting.

We are _____, joining Jesus on His mission, as kingdom agents engaged in kingdom work.

We _____ the kingdom because we live in a world with no concept of kingdoms.

"The kingdom of God has come near" is a _____ statement.

The kingdom of God is already _____.

"inaugurated"—_____
"eschatology"—the _____ of all things

The kingdom of God is _____, but not _____.

Jesus speaks of the kingdom of God using _____.

The Bible never _____ the kingdom of God, but it frequently _____ it using parables.

Discuss the teaching with your group using the questions below.

1. Were you surprised to see how important the kingdom of God was in Jesus' teaching? Why or why not?

2. Do you think that most Christians assign the same level of importance to the kingdom as other spiritual issues? If not the kingdom, what spiritual issues tend to dominate?

3. In what ways might our spiritual lives and development be different if we gave greater thought and attention to the kingdom?

4. In what sense is the kingdom already here? In what sense is the kingdom not yet here? Why do you think it's important to understand this "already but not yet" kingdom dynamic?

5. Why do you think the kingdom of God is never defined in Scripture?

6. What do you think it means to "seek first the kingdom"? How have people misunderstood that command throughout history?

7. This week you will individually study more of these kingdom dynamics. What is one specific way your group might pray for you this week in regard to your understanding of the kingdom of God?

Close with prayer.

LAUNCHING OUT

Scripture Memory

> "Seek first the kingdom of God and His righteousness, and all these things will be provided for you." MATTHEW 6:33

Kingdom Seeking

* Prepare for your in-depth study of kingdom parables by reading Matthew 13:1-58.
* Pray that the Lord would help you to see the beauty and priority of His kingdom.
* Carry a journal with you all week. Write specific instances when you see evidence of the kingdom of God.

Video sessions are available for purchase at *www.lifeway.com/sk*

kingdom perspective

There once was a great king who ruled a vast, faraway land with grace and mercy. He was the most rare sort of ruler who, despite his tremendous power and resources, was constantly concerned with the good of his people. A day did not go by when the king did not stroll the streets of his towns alongside the people who trusted him for their care.

Those were wonderful days in the kingdom, days when people loved and believed in the righteous reign of their leader. But, as often happens during such times, great calamity lurked in the shadows.

Though the king was good and kind, there was another ruler who resented his reign. The great enemy of the king was poisoned by self-obsession and convinced that he should be the true ruler of the kingdom. But how would one go about overthrowing a ruler so powerful and mighty as the king? It was a tricky business. But the enemy was as crafty as the king was good, and he hatched a plan.

Rather than a direct assault against the king, he would begin a systematic process of internal strife that he hoped would throw the land into disarray. He would create doubt concerning the goodness of the king, while attempting to usurp his power. And so it was that the enemy moved inside of the kingdom, slowly but surely creating a spirit of discontent among the people. Whispers began. Uncertainty crept in. And soon the citizens of the kingdom were not so sure that they wanted to be subjects of their king any longer. ...

DAY 1 kingdom mistaken

The kingdom is plastered on page after page of Scripture. However, despite its prominence, there remains a tremendous amount of confusion about what is the kingdom. When it is. Who its king is. And even why the kingdom exists at all.

It would be easier and simpler for us to not worry much about kingdom issues, assuming that because we've been in church for years, God's kingdom will just take care of itself. However, we do not have that luxury if we want to take seriously the red-lettered words of Jesus in the New Testament. To love and believe in Jesus means you must love, believe in, and pursue His kingdom.

When Jesus arrived and began His public ministry, one of the first things that He declared was: "The kingdom of God has come near" (Mark 1:15). He came to establish the kingdom of God on the earth and to create a kingdom people.

Jesus' message should have resonated greatly with the nation of Israel. However a problem arose as Jesus began explaining the nature of His kingdom. Matthew describes the early days of Jesus' ministry. Read in 4:23-25 how he describes Jesus' teaching on the kingdom:

> "Jesus was going all over Galilee, teaching in their synagogues, preaching the good news of the kingdom, and healing every disease and sickness among the people. Then the news about Him spread throughout Syria. So they brought to Him all those who were afflicted, those suffering from various diseases and intense pains, the demon-possessed, the epileptics, and the paralytics. And He healed them. Large crowds followed Him from Galilee, Decapolis, Jerusalem, Judea, and beyond the Jordan." *MT 4:23-25*

What three words come to mind first when you hear the phrase "kingdom of God"?

What do you know about Israel at the starting Time of Jesus' ministry?.

- Poor - Impoverished   weak
- Under Roman Control - Taxes Freedom
- 400 years of waiting
- Fractured Politically - Herodians, Zealots,
* Fractured Spiritually - Pharisee / Sad.*

Do you consider the kingdom of God an important subject? Why or why not?

Why does Matthew say Jesus preached "the good news of the kingdom"? What changes in your mind and heart regarding the kingdom of God when you read this description?

Before this point in his Gospel, Matthew recorded only a few of Jesus' words. He narrated how Jesus rebuffed Satan during the temptations in Matthew 4, but the first words of Jesus in His public proclamation were "Repent, because the kingdom of heaven has come near!" (Matt. 4:17). This must have been music to the ears of His audience! Or maybe not.

Do you think the people would have welcomed such a message? Why or why not?

How do you imagine those people interpreted Jesus' message about the kingdom?

The people had been waiting for centuries. They had suffered under multiple oppressors. The prophecies with which they had often encouraged one another were clear—a king was going to come and deliver them from bondage.

Read one of these prophecies for yourself in Isaiah 9:2-7. Based on this passage, what kind of Messiah do you think the people were expecting?

Prophecy of a King

At the time of Christ's ministry on earth, the Jews were under the thumb of the Roman Empire. Palestine was an occupied land. When they looked to the future and the deliverance of God, they expected their Messiah to break off their Roman bonds. They were looking for a military commander and political ruler who would wipe out His enemies, set up the kingdom right then, and rule—not just Israel, but the world—from Jerusalem. They expected the kingdom to come in a revolution, an overthrow of Rome and any other oppressors that stood in their way. But God had a different plan in mind, and they never saw it coming.

The king was born in a backwoods town called Bethlehem. He grew up in an inauspicious manner, without pomp and ceremony, until He burst onto the scene preaching about the kingdom of God.

This challenged the dreams and assumptions of the Jewish people.

Can you sympathize with the Israel? Have you ever expected God to act in one way only to be surprised by His choice? How so?

Does knowing that Jesus grew up in obscurity give you insight into the nature of the kingdom of God? If so, what does it mean?

How do you think Jesus would have defined the kingdom of God?

Jesus' unlikely birth reveals the surprising nature of the kingdom of God. It's not a political domain but a spiritual kingdom. It wasn't brought forth by a conquering general but by a wandering teacher. And at His birth the angels announced that He is the Chosen One who will save their people from their enemy. The enemy from which He saves, however, is sin, not Rome. The oppression from which He delivers is the Devil's, not Caesar's.

Tragically, the very people who should have been the first in line to greet the coming kingdom were those who missed its advent. Many people during the days of Jesus were so committed to their opinions of how God should work, how His kingdom should function, and what form His deliverance should take that they missed the Son of God in their midst. They saw, heard, and touched God in the flesh, yet did not recognize Him.

Could it be possible that the same thing is happening today? Could it be that we are missing the good news of the kingdom of God because we are committed to our version of that kingdom rather than the biblical one?

Reflect on that last statement. What are some potential versions of Jesus and the kingdom in which we might choose to believe?

How can we ensure that our view of the kingdom is aligned with Jesus' view of the kingdom?

All around us, there are conflicting messages about the nature of the kingdom of God. Some argue that it's about being healthy and wealthy. Others say it's already come and gone. And some say that it will only be seen in a perfect reign of Jesus someday long in the future.

The danger we face in looking at the kingdom is the same today as it was in the past: We might be so committed to the conquering general that we miss the baby in the manger.

DAY 2 kingdom nature

The Jews waited for it. Jesus was committed to it. Confusion surrounds it, even today. So what exactly does the Bible mean when it talks about the kingdom of God? Fortunately, that's a question Matthew works to answer throughout his Gospel. Look at Matthew 9:35:

> "Jesus went to all the towns and villages, teaching in their synagogues, preaching the good news of the kingdom, and healing every disease and every sickness."

What three things did Jesus do according to this passage?

1.

2.

3.

Teaching, preaching, and healing. Scripture sets up this pattern in Jesus' ministry, and all three of these aspects of His ministry are meant to announce the good news of the kingdom. Jesus is preaching, teaching, and healing: teaching the Jews what the kingdom life looks like, preaching to all the good news of the kingdom, and healing the sick and raising the dead to life to demonstrate that He has the power of the kingdom. In His teaching, preaching, and healing, He proclaims that He is the King of kings and the Lord of lords. That means we can look to both the words and actions of Jesus in the Book of Matthew to learn the nature of this kingdom.

What specific stories can you recall when Jesus taught about or demonstrated the nature of the kingdom of God?

Why would Jesus use the methods of teaching, preaching, and healing to communicate His message about the kingdom? Are these merely effective communication techniques? Or, do they suggest something about the nature of the kingdom of God?

Though the people of His day eagerly awaited the kingdom of heaven, Jesus' ministry can be described as a re-education process, for He worked to correct mistaken ideas about the nature of that kingdom. One of the most basic misperceptions Jesus sought to correct involved the mission of the kingdom of heaven.

Read John 18:36. What circumstances led to Jesus' statements in this verse?

What does His answer reveal about the nature of the kingdom?

It's a pretty specific statement and bad news to all those who were looking for Jesus to take control of the government and be the political and military champion of Israel. According to Jesus, the kingdom is a spiritual kingdom.

The kingdom isn't formed by borders. Its territory wasn't decided by natural landmarks or treaties. It isn't geopolitical in nature. The kingdom of God is spiritual in nature. But that's not all.

Read Luke 17:20-21. What does this passage indicate about the kingdom of God?

Do you tend to think of the kingdom as a present reality or a future reality? Why?

According to Jesus, the kingdom of God "has come near" (Matt. 10:7). It's as B.B. Warfield, the famous Princeton theologian, wrote in the 1920s:

> "When our Lord came down to earth He drew heaven with Him. The signs which accompanied His ministry were but the trailing clouds of glory which He brought from heaven, which is His home. The number of miracles which He wrought may easily be underrated. It has been said that in effect He banished disease and death from Palestine for the three years of His ministry. ...

quote

> "One hem but of the garment that He wore
> Could medicine whole countries of their pain;
> One touch of that pale hand could life restore."[1]

Rephrase Warfield's statement above in your own words.

21

Jesus declared that the kingdom of God had come. We see from Scripture that the kingdom of God was among them for one reason and one reason alone: *Jesus was there.*

With Jesus comes the kingdom. Jesus was not only teaching and preaching this good news—He was demonstrating the present reality of the kingdom through healing.

How would healing demonstrate the kingdom?

In His ministry, Jesus taught about the kingdom of God, but He also provided a glimpse inside the nature and power of the kingdom in His compassionate acts of healing. At the end of time, in the kingdom of God for all eternity, we are promised that there will be no more tears, sickness, or pain. In His miraculous acts of healing, Jesus testified to the hope and power of the fullness of the kingdom and to the reality of its presence in the world through Him.

One day, Jesus will be the recognized king, and all will joyfully submit to His rule. If we are following Jesus, we must seek to bring about the kingdom of God too. Because Jesus emphasized its spiritual nature in His teaching and showed the physical component to it with His healing, we must engage in both.

We should be seeking to demonstrate the power of the kingdom at work through the people of God. That's not to say we need to begin "healing ministries" all over the land. It means that part of seeking the kingdom of God is sharing about the kingdom and showing the reality of the kingdom at work each day.

What are some tangible ways you might demonstrate the kingdom of God to your community?

DAY 3 kingdom changes

In the kingdom of God, everything is different. Because we are citizens of this new kingdom, we have a different agenda and a different mission than the kingdoms of the world. Our citizenship belongs to a different kingdom because we serve a different King.

In short, everything changes in the kingdom.

Jesus' first statements about this kingdom told us it would require change. Remember, when He declared that the kingdom of God is near in Matthew 4:17, He said first, "Repent." This word basically means *change the direction of your life.*

We enter into the kingdom of God when we accept by faith that Jesus died for our sins. When we believe in Him, an enormous change takes place. We move from being children of darkness to children of light, from being the enemies of God to coheirs with Christ, and from being strangers to God's kingdom to His ambassadors.

Jesus' message of kingdom entrance is clear: "Repent, because the kingdom of heaven has come near!" (Matt. 4:17). There are three important parts to His statement that we should examine.

First of all, entering the kingdom requires a changed heart. That changed heart is expressed in the call to repent.

Define *repent* in your own words.

When is the last time you heard a sermon or someone talk about repentance?

23

The Greek word for repentance used in the Bible is *metanoya*. It means *to change one's mind; to have another mind*. The root word, *meta*, is the same one that forms the word metamorphosis. Repentance, then, is a change of mind as dramatic as metamorphosis is a change of shape. Repentance transforms your mind the way a caterpillar is transformed into a butterfly.

In what sense does repentance call for a change of mind?

What do you need to change your mind about when you repent?

We see this over and over again related to the kingdom of God. Jesus didn't just call for repentance generally. He called people specifically to "Repent, *because the kingdom of heaven is near!*"

We are called to repent of sin, of the world's way of thinking, valuing, and doing, but we repent because of the kingdom's nearness. See, repentance isn't only a change of mind *from* sin; it's a change of mind *toward* the kingdom.

Paul refers to two expressions of remorse or grief in 2 Corinthians 7:8-10. He acknowledges that people can and often do experience grief over certain decisions or actions. But, mere grief is not sufficient, for there are two types of grief. One leads to death while the other one leads to life. Godly grief leads us to repentance and salvation, because it directs our lives to be for God and His kingdom purposes.

The picture of the two steps of repentance from sin and to God is captured well in Hebrews 12:1-2 where the writer illustrates this concept using a sporting event.

> **Read Hebrews 12:1-2. What are the two sides of repentance in these verses?**

> **What are we meant to lay aside?**

> **What are we meant to focus on instead?**

Do you see it? When repentance is laid out in Scripture, the idea is that a person is headed one way. But the person doesn't just stop going that direction—they turn and go another way. The change of mind is from sin to Jesus and His kingdom. That's what a changed heart is all about.

Entering the kingdom of God also means a change in loyalty. Just after His announcement of the kingdom coming near in Matthew 4:17, Jesus encountered a group of fishermen on the beach. His call in Matthew 4:19 was simple: "Follow Me."

> **Read Matthew 4:19-20. How did the fishermen respond?**

> **Do you think there is any significance to the fact that they left their nets? Why or Why not?**

To an ancient fisherman, nothing was more valuable than a good net. It was an essential piece of gear for their livelihood. The net was used to put food on the table and care for one's family. It symbolized a fisherman's entire life—a mark of identity. Yet here we see a group leaving all that behind to follow Jesus in His kingdom mission.

The call isn't so different today. If we want to be about the business of the kingdom, our loyalties must change. We have to drop our nets. This is an issue to which Jesus brings extreme clarity. In His mind, there are two starkly different agendas a person might have. On the one hand your agenda can be built around the kingdom of heaven and the business of God. Otherwise, your agenda can be built around the kingdom of yourself. It is one or the other but certainly not both.

With what specific areas of your life do you struggle the most in having a kingdom loyalty?

How are you currently pursuing the kingdom agenda in those areas?

What might need to change so the agenda of God's kingdom becomes the priority of your life?

Finally, entering the kingdom means you live within a tension.

Jesus said, "Repent, because the kingdom of heaven has come *near*!" (Matt. 4:17, emphasis added). This raises the question: how near is the kingdom of heaven? We find ourselves in a tension at this point. If the kingdom of heaven has come near through the coming of Jesus, then why are there so many things wrong in the world? Why are there so many orphans? And diseases? And impoverished people? Why is there so much suffering and oppression? It's because the kingdom is both *now* and *not yet*.

A lesson from American history will help us understand here. As World War II came to a close, there were two important dates. The first one occurred on June 6th, 1944. History remembers it as "D-day."

what do we call these dates

As a part of Operation Overlord, the United States and its allies landed on the beach of Normandy, France. It was the beginning of the end of the war. Yet the war in Europe didn't end until more than a year later on May 7th, 1945, also known as "VE-day."

Despite the fact that the victory at Normandy effectively broke the back of the Axis powers, the war didn't officially end until months later. In fact, more people died in between those dates than any other period of the war. It was dark and difficult, but the end had begun. It was inaugurated June 6th, 1944, but the end wasn't consummated until May 7th, 1945. That's the difference between D-day and VE-day.

How does this illustration relate to the kingdom of God?

In terms of the kingdom, what was D-day? What will be VE-day?

That's not a perfect parallel, but when the kingdom of God arrived in the person of Jesus, it came near. But, it will not be fully realized until Jesus returns at the end of time. The church is left to live between the times. We are called to advance God's kingdom even as we wait for Jesus' return.

kingdom priorities

Everything changes when you enter the kingdom of God. The heart, loyalty, priorities—it's all different. It must be so if we are to be kingdom representatives in the in between time—the time between the cross and the return of Jesus.

All of those changes add up to a radical readjustment of priorities for those in the kingdom. It seems obvious, yet most of us still struggle to have a kingdom-driven agenda for our lives.

What would you say are the top three priorities in the kingdom of the world?

1.

2.

3.

What should be the top three priorities in the kingdom of God?

1.

2.

3.

Why do you think Christians sometimes struggle with having a kingdom-driven agenda?

You'd be hard-pressed to find a topic that was more prioritized to Jesus than the kingdom. Though we often think of Jesus' teaching being about heaven, hell, money, or sex, He emphasized the kingdom far more than these other subjects.

Depending on how you count, here are more than 80 references to the kingdom of God in the Gospels of Matthew, Mark, and Luke. The Book of Matthew alone contains more than 30. Just from the sheer volume of times Jesus taught about the kingdom, we can't help but see just how important it was to Him during His earthly ministry.

Jesus not only lead off His public ministry with statements about the kingdom but in His most famous sermon, commonly called the Sermon on the Mount, He called for a radical commitment to a kingdom way of life.

> **Read Matthew 6:33. What do you think it means to seek the kingdom of God?**

> **Read the surrounding passage, Matthew 6:25-34.
> How do you think seeking the kingdom links to Jesus'
> encouragement to not worry?**

Most of us see our priorities in this section of Scripture, though not in verse 33. Instead, we are those who seek what we will eat. Or wear. Or earn. We spend a good deal of time worrying about these parts of life: What if my job is down-sized? What if my children aren't provided for? What if my spouse gets sick?

The truth is that whatever worries us is probably a good gauge of our priorities. That is to say, if we spend time and energy worrying about something, chances are we are holding that thing in fairly high esteem.

If you are one of the people who don't worry much, it probably means you are more optimistic and hopeful. So, what you hope for may also indicate what your priorities are.

What do you spend your time dreaming about? What are you saving your money to purchase?

What does that reveal about your priorities?

As kingdom people, God is calling us to live by the values of His kingdom—values that should shape every aspect of our lives. We are called to be so single-minded concerning the kingdom that everything else should pale in comparison. The promise from Jesus is that if we have kingdom priorities, then we really don't have to worry about anything else. God will provide in all other areas.

Is that promise difficult for you to believe? Why or why not?

What specific areas of your life would have to be refocused in order for you to seek the kingdom of God?

What do you think it means for you to seek God's kingdom in the following areas of life:

Your occupation:

Your family:

Your friendships:

Your church:

Though we'll spend the remainder of this study discussing these attributes of the kingdom and how to seek them in everyday life, it's clear from the outset that a kingdom-driven agenda is very different. It's subversive to the priorities and kingdom of the world. To seek priorities of the kingdom is, in effect, making the commitment to zag when then kingdom of the world zigs. It's a conscious choice to swim against the current, to go against the flow. It's a determined spirit to look for opportunities to subvert the status quo by living out the heart, loyalty, and priorities of God's kingdom.

It is these values of the kingdom that will separate the followers of Jesus from the rest of the world.

Consider your current life agenda. How different is that agenda from the agenda of the world around you? Why is that so?

DAY 5 kingdom stories

Living according to the kingdom of God is mission-critical for followers of Christ. Jesus believed it to be so, and we might wonder then how He would go about communicating these essential truths to His followers. We receive our answer in Matthew 13.

Read Matthew 13:1-3. Why do you think Jesus chose the form of parables to communicate truths about the kingdom?

What is effective about that methodology?

Interestingly enough, however, Jesus never gave a firm definition of the kingdom of God. As much as we might want Him to straightforwardly say, "Here's what I mean by the kingdom. It's a paragraph long, but you would do well to memorize it." He did not do this. Rather, He used words to paint a picture of the kingdom.

He said that the kingdom of heaven is like a woman who has lost a coin, or a shepherd who lost a sheep, or a father who lost a son. It's like a pearl of great price or a seed falling into different kinds of soil. Through these pictures, we get a picture of the kingdom of God but not a definition.

These pictures are called *parables*. A parable, according to C.H. Dodd in *The Parables of the Kingdom*, is "a metaphor or simile drawn from nature or common life, arresting the hearer by its vividness or strangeness, and leaving the mind in sufficient doubt about its precise application to tease it into active thought."[2] These pictures are meant to give understanding to those who have ears to hear the good news of the kingdom and confuse those who don't have ears to hear. Jesus tells these parables to give understanding and paint a robust picture of the kingdom. They may leave us asking, "Well, what exactly does it mean?"

They may leave us thinking about the nature of the kingdom. But, they are not intended to confuse those who want to hear the good news.

> **What is the most interesting part of the definition of a parable to you?**

> **What value is there in leading the hearer of such stories to thinking, rather than to specific answers?**

Making things even more interesting is the fact that Jesus' method of communication changes in Matthew 13. Up until that point, He had been more straightforward in His teaching. He had talked about His identity. He had preached the Sermon on the Mount. Then He began speaking in word pictures, painting full and glorious pictures of the presence and mission of the kingdom in our day.

Understandably, His disciples were a little confused so they asked Jesus, "Why do You speak to them in parables?" (Matt. 13:10).

> **Read Jesus' response in Matthew 13:11. What were His reasons for speaking in parables?**

Jesus used the word "secrets" in His response. The kingdom, then, is far from obvious. It's countercultural, even foolish, to those who are not a part of it. It's a subversive kingdom, one in which secrets are entrusted to its citizens but one that is meant to stay under the radar, gaining ground and followers as time passes. More and more people discover the secrets of the kingdom, and when they do, their loyalty changes to the kingdom of God.

What are some ways you have seen the subversive nature of the kingdom of God at work, transforming the priorities of those around you?

Speaking in parables allowed Jesus' disciples to understand the secrets of the kingdom, but it also prevented others from knowing those secrets. That's another part of what Jesus said in Matthew 13:11—that "it has not been given to them."

Does this strike you as strange? Why or why not?

Why might Jesus not want some people to know the secrets of the kingdom?

There is no easy answer here. Perhaps it's because some of His hearers would reject—or had already rejected—the kingdom Jesus was bringing. Perhaps it was because God was already at work in the hearts of the disciples but not in the hearts of others. For whatever the reason, these parables served as a point of separation for true disciples.

Finally, Jesus spoke in parables in order to fulfill the prophecy that He would do so.

Read Matthew 13:13-15. What do you think Jesus meant when He quoted this passage from Isaiah?

How had the hearts of certain people of His day grown callous?

Speaking about how the hyperreligious people of His day—those too busy seeking their own achievement to notice the true kingdom of God—Jesus hearkened back to the days of Isaiah when similar things were going on. He was surrounded by people who were so preoccupied with religious activity that they were blinded to the truth of God's kingdom.

Could it be that the same thing is happening today? We live in a world where spiritual and religious people abound. People hear teaching about the kingdom of God and pay little heed because they go to church, have prayed a prayer, or maybe even been baptized. Perhaps they even give to charity or the local church. Because of all these things, these people think they're inside the kingdom.

Jesus stepped into the middle of the religiosity of the Pharisees of His day to say that the secrets of the kingdom were passing them by. Their hearts were cal-loused toward the things of the kingdom, and we know this because they missed these secrets. Does He have a similar message for the church today? Are we missing the secrets of the kingdom?

Let's make sure we are kingdom people. Changed people. New people. And get ready, because the secrets of the kingdom are at hand!

1. Benjamin B. Warfield, *Counterfeit Miracles*, (New York: Charles Scribner's Sons, 1918), 3. Available from the Internet: *http://books.google.com*.
2. C.H. Dodd, *The Parables of the Kingdom*, quoted in Craig Blomberg, *Interpreting the Parables* (Downers Grove, Illinois: InterVarsity Press, 1990), 34–35.

subversive
kingdom

kingdom growing

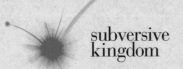

SESSION 2

GETTING STARTED

1. Based on your individual study, is there any particular part of your understanding of the kingdom of God that is being challenged?

2. The parable of the sower is a well-known story. What are some specific questions you have about that particular parable?

3. What do you think was Jesus' main point in telling this story?

PRESSING IN

Watch the teaching segment from the DVD using the viewer guide below.

Characteristics of the Sower:

1. The sower sows ... _____.

2. The sower sows ... _____.

3. The sower sows ... _____.

New Testament Soils:

1. The hard soil: _____

2. The rocky soil: The rich young ruler

3. The soil of thorns: _____

We want to be people where the _____ of the kingdom takes deep root.

Bad _____ often make good _____.

When the seed is sown in you, you become a _____.

An ambassador is a high-ranking diplomatic official sent to _____ the ways of another land.

Discuss the teaching with your group using the questions below.

1. What are some specific ways you see God embodying the characteristics of the sower?

2. How confident are you in the word of God to do its work when sown? What experiences in your past have led to that kind of confidence?

3. Describe some characteristics of the hearts of the people represented by different kinds of soil in this passage.

4. Which of those soils best represents your own heart right now?

5. Has that always been the case? Describe a time in your life when your heart was like a different kind of soil.

6. What kinds of circumstances have made your heart change?

7. How does the role of ambassador relate to sowing the seed of the kingdom of God?

Close with prayer.

LAUNCHING OUT

Scripture Memory

> "The one planting and the one watering
> are one in purpose, and each will receive
> his own reward according to his labor. For
> we are God's coworkers. You are God's
> field, God's building."

1 CORINTHIANS 3:8-9

Kingdom Seeking

* Pray specifically for the people in your own life who represent the different kinds of soil in the parable of the sower.
* Do you know all your neighbors? This week, make an effort to meet one of them you haven't yet.
* Look for ways in your new relationship that you might scatter the seed of the God's Word.

Video sessions are available for purchase at *www.lifeway.com/sk*

kingdom growing

It's difficult to believe that a people who had been so loved might so quickly abandon the one who always had been faithful to care for them. But the great enemy struck.

His lie was simple, yet deviously conceived. He spread it throughout the towns of the kingdom, and the people believed it one by one. The lie started with a simple question, "Does your king really love you?" Of course, the people at first answered with a resounding yes. But the more they thought about it, the less certain they became.

If the king loved them, then why were there rules of conduct for life in the kingdom? Were they just subjects to be ruled? True, they had all they needed, but there was more to be had, and there were aspects of life the king had forbidden.

Slowly but surely, the people began to desire to live outside of his rule. They were caught up in visions of freedom—with the idea that they were better equipped to chart their destinies than their ruler. Whispers of rebellion turned into meetings of protest. People began to openly question the king and the kingdom and invited others to open their minds as well.

The great enemy watched all this change with glee. The king watched with sadness. And soon, the people cast off the rule of their king, convinced that they could rule themselves. Their king, who once so freely walked alongside his people, became a distant memory.

DAY 1 kingdom sowing

Nobody ever said Jesus was an expert in public relations. Many times in His ministry, people were ready to march to Jerusalem with Jesus on their shoulders. "Declare the revolution!" people must have urged. They wanted Jesus to overthrow the political establishment, and they were ready to take up arms if necessary to follow Him.

But instead of rallying the crowds, Jesus was in the habit of dispersing them with difficult teachings and strange stories. After one such happening, Scripture records, "From that moment many of His disciples turned back and no longer accompanied Him" (John 6:66).

> **Why do you think Jesus thinned out the crowds of those who followed Him?**

> **Would it not have made more sense to gather larger and larger crowds so that more people could hear the message?**

Matthew 13 marks the point in Jesus' ministry when He became cryptic and mysterious in ways that He had not been before. Prior to this moment, Jesus had been pretty straightforward. He'd given the Sermon on the Mount. He'd talked about His identity. Then suddenly, in Matthew 13:3, we find this:

"He told them many things in parables."

Why the sudden shift to obscurity? And why at this particular point in His ministry? The key to understanding the shift in His teaching emphasis is in chapter 12.

Scan through Matthew 12. How would you describe the mood of this chapter?

What does Jesus address in His teaching?

Make a list of the different groups of people represented in this chapter.

Jesus stirred up controversy in Matthew 12. The Pharisees were charging Him with demon possession. Jesus was pointing at the most important landmark in the life of the Jewish nation—the temple—and claiming that He was greater than even that. It all got to be a little too much for some of His listeners.

As Matthew 12 closes, Jesus' family decided they needed to rein Him in a little bit.

Read Matthew 12:46-50. Put yourself in the place of Jesus' mother and brothers. What would you have said to Him if you had been one of them?

At first glance, we might think the same thing that Jesus' brothers probably did: *Who does this guy think He is?* It seems like an arrogant and self-important way to respond. But even in this situation, Jesus was teaching an important lesson about the kingdom.

In fact, this event is what specifically led to Jesus' transition into the use of parables concerning the kingdom of God. Here's how Jesus' family and the upcoming parables fit together: The kingdom is subversive. It's secret. And even those closest to Jesus couldn't understand it unless their eyes were opened.

This is what the first kingdom parable is about. It shows how and why all the other parables of the kingdom would be received or not received among the people.

> **Read Matthew 13:1-9,18-23. Fill in the space below with what each part of the parable represents:**
>
> **Sower:**
>
>
> **Seed:**
>
>
> **Soil:**
>
>
> **Crop:**

In just a few, well-chosen words, Jesus delivered a verbal picture of how the kingdom of God takes root in a person's heart. He described the generous nature of the sower, who threw seed everywhere He could. He talked about the different types of soil that may—or may not—accept the good seed. And He talked about the differing results when the seed lands on those different kinds of soil.

This is the kingdom of God in you. In me. In us. It begins small. Not everyone understands it. But for a few, the seed of the kingdom takes root and grows. And grows. And grows. And much fruit is borne.

Do you think the message of the kingdom has found fertile ground in you? Why or why not?

What does "fertile ground" look like in a person?

What do you need to do to prepare the soil of your heart for the seed that God wants to sow there?

DAY 2 the seed of the kingdom

There stood Jesus. His family was outside wanting a word with Him. Rather than speaking with them, Jesus changed His focus of communication. The nature of the kingdom was being displayed before Him, and He acknowledged its subversion. It seemed that not even those closest to Him—His mother and brothers—were yet able to understand the kind of kingdom He was bringing about. They certainly wouldn't be the last to not understand.

Matthew 13 is a parable about this reality—that there are secrets of the kingdom of God, and not everyone will understand what it is meant to be. According to Jesus, the beginning of this kingdom is like a farmer scattering seed.

> **Look again at Matthew 13:1-9. Jesus began with the words, "Consider the sower" (v. 3). When you consider the sower, what picture comes to mind?**

> **Does the way he scattered seed mean anything to you? Why or why not?**

> **Why might that manner of scattering be surprising?**

What does the seed represent in the parable?

Due to our familiarity with cornfields in Iowa or soybeans in south Georgia, we tend to think of planting in terms of large, flat fields with seemingly perfect, geometrically engineered rows of crops. While there may have been some large farms like that in first-century Palestine, much of their planting was done on small homesteads, often on hillsides.

Many times, footpaths wove in and out of the planting areas. Because they used donkeys to plow, rather than powerful tractors, many rocks did not get moved. In Jesus' day, the end result was that a farmer scattering seed would routinely hit all four types of soil in the same general area.

The farmer's actions were not random, though they might seem so to us. Scattering was the method best suited for spreading seed in this context.

What does the manner of the farmer's sowing reveal about the farmer's character?

What specifically does that indicate about the character of God?

Here is a farmer who is willing to throw the seed far and wide. He knows full well that not all of it will take hold and grow, but that doesn't stop him from freely distributing it. You might even say that the seed goes out to the "whosoever" of the soil, for maybe, just maybe, some of it will grow. Apparently, he has the seed in such abundance and is so confident of its quality that he's willing to waste some—even much—just in case there might be some good soil amidst the rocks and on the hard ground.

The seed scattered in the parable is the word of the kingdom. Luke calls it "the word of God" (Luke 8:11), and Mark calls it simply "the word" (Mark 4:14). That's where the kingdom begins—with the scattering of the word of God. And like the farmer, God does not withhold His word. He sends it out far and wide in a variety of ways.

> **Read Psalm 19:1-4. According to this passage, how is the word of God scattered?**

> **How far and wide does it go?**

> **What are some other ways the word is scattered?**

Nature, the testimonies of Christians, copies of the Bible itself—these are examples of the seed of the kingdom going out. The word of God is dispersed freely but also confidently.

> Read Hebrews 4:12-13. Make a list below of the words used to describe the word of God.

> Recall a personal experience when the Bible has been living and active to you. Write about that experience below.

The word of God continues to be scattered. It's true that the scattering does not always yield kingdom change where it falls, but we need to understand clearly: The problem isn't with the seed. It never is. The message of the kingdom of God is penetrating and powerful. It's complete in and of itself.

> Read 1 Corinthians 3:5-7. What was Paul's main point in this passage?

"God gave the growth" (v. 6). God is the power behind the seed. Paul's implication to the Corinthian church was that it was irrelevant how they had received the word. Some had received the word as Paul had sown it, others when Apollos had scattered it. It did not matter; it was God who had given the growth.

There is nothing wrong with the word of God, and to live in the kingdom we must be armed with this confidence. For the kingdom to grow in our hearts and eventually in the world around us, we must eagerly receive the seed of the word of God and allow its power to produce abundant kingdom fruit in our lives.

What one word best describes how you view God's word? Why?

Do you think most of us have confidence in God's word? How do you know?

How would our lives be different if we had unshakable confidence in His word?

What is one way that you might develop a greater confidence in God's word today?

DAY 3 the bad soil

With the kind of reckless abandon demonstrated by the farmer in Jesus' story, no one could rightly expect that all the seed the farmer scattered would eventually bear fruit. Handfuls of seed were thrown out in a seemingly indiscriminate way, and Jesus acknowledged that not all of it grew roots.

Birds ate some of the seed before it had a chance to grow. Some fell among rocks, and though the plants that sprang up looked promising, they eventually withered in the heat due to the shallowness of their roots. Still others grew up alongside thorns but then were choked out.

Not all of the seed bore fruit. In each case, the determining factor of the strength and stability of the crop had to do with the quality of the soil. The sower is the same. The seed is the same. Only the soil is different.

> **Read again Matthew 13:1-9. In this parable, what does the soil represent?**

> **What one word would you use to describe each type of soil?**

> **Soil 1:**

> **Soil 2:**

> **Soil 3:**

The seed had different results in each instance depending on where it landed. Some of the seed landed on unprepared ground. According to Matthew 13:4, the seed landed on the ground along the side of the road or perhaps on the path itself. Horse hooves, people's shoes, and chariot wheels had packed down the dirt, resulting in hardened soil completely unsuitable for planting.

Read Matthew 13:19. What type of person is the first type of soil meant to represent?

Who in your life might you liken to this type of soil?

The problem with this hard, unprepared ground is that it makes it impossible for the seed to really ever take root. The seed isn't in the soil; it's merely on the pathway.

One widely held interpretation of the pathway kind of soil is that it represents the unconverted heart. In this understanding, the word does not penetrate the heart, bringing life and transformation. Instead, the seed lies on top of the hardened heart, with its limitless power untapped. Because it grows no roots, it is easy for the birds to swoop down and eat it up. Jesus likens this to Satan's destructive work (see Mark 4:15).

Like the soil of the heart, our hearts can be hard and resistant. Our own sinful nature and desires, the temptation of evil one, and the world around us can serve to make the soil of our hearts very, very hard. We get busy with work, busy with family, busy being entertained—all the while the seed keeps falling on us. We desire money, security, image, power, and pleasure, and seed falls on us. We simply don't have the time and desire to receive it. Jesus' language for this type of situation is that "the birds came and ate them up" (Matt 13:4).

What hope is there for that kind of heart?

What kinds of circumstances might God use to break up the unprepared ground of people's hearts?

Have you personally experienced that breaking of your heart? How so?

Paul says the only hope is that Spirit will open the eyes of our heart so that we can see the truth and goodness of the gospel, for the evil one blinds the heart of the unbelievers (see Eph. 1:18).

God uses circumstances and people in our lives to awaken us to the truth of the gospel. Often it's only through tragedy that the hard ground of people's hearts is broken up. When confronted by some life-changing circumstance, all the aspects of life that make us too busy to pay attention to the seed of the kingdom no longer seem so important. It is through the breaking up of hardened hearts that we see the redemptive purpose of God in tragic circumstances.

But that's not the only kind of soil Jesus mentioned. The second type is the rocky ground.

Read Matthew 13:20-21. What type of person does the rocky ground represent?

Who in your life might you liken to this type of soil?

What ways may this condition be true about your own heart right now?

This response to the seed of the kingdom is heartbreaking because it's initially so full of promise. This person receives the seed with great joy and excitement. There is hope in the family of God. And yet that excitement is short-lived because of the shallowness of the soil.

Sometimes in church we are quick to point out the great benefits of the kingdom: the security of eternal life, hope in the present, peace that passes understanding. But we can't forget that the call to follow Christ is a call to die. There is no fence-sitting in the kingdom. Either Jesus has our all or He has nothing. The seed comes and takes a little root, but it doesn't last because the pressures of life, the immorality of the culture, or the call of the world is simply too much. This is not a case of a person losing the salvation of the kingdom of God—it's a case of failing to truly commit to the kingdom in the first place.

Read Matthew 13:7,22. What type of person does this soil describe?

What's the difference between this person and the person described by the rocky soil?

While similar, this type of soil fails to produce fruit from the seed for a slightly different reason than the previous one. In this case, Jesus specified "the worries of this age and the seduction of wealth choke the word" (v. 22). Perhaps this soil is the most troubling of all because it fits so many people we know.

In other words, Jesus was saying that all the things we own and our daily lives can get in the way of our relationship with Him. These are the thorns that choke the life out of the word of the kingdom. Sadly, this is the place where many of us have found ourselves—knowing we should be living differently and yet so caught up in the daily grind and the constant pursuit of more and more stuff that we barely give the things of the kingdom a second thought.

How do we respond to these realities? Do we just shake our heads in pity? Do we look down our noses, judging the soil of the hearts of those around us? Or do we continue to pray to God, the great sower and the Lord of the harvest, to do the impossible? To turn thorny, rocky, hard places into soil that can receive the word of the kingdom?

It must be the latter, as we continue to trust in Him for the increase of His kingdom.

Who specifically can you pray for today, that God would change the soil of their heart?

Could that person be you? Do you see your own heart in any of these kinds of soil? If so, pray that God would change the soil of your heart too.

DAY 4 kingdom soil

"Others fell on good ground and produced a crop: some 100, some 60, and some 30 times what was sown" (Matt. 13:8).

In this kingdom parable, the soil determined the results. The same seed fell. We have no indication that there was any difference in quality of the seed, nor any other condition to make these particular seeds more fruitful than the others. Nothing except the soil.

Read Matthew 13:23. What does the good soil represent?

What character traits come to mind when you think about a person like this verse describes?

Notice that the person of the good soil "hears" and "understands." What's the difference between hearing and understanding?

Many people heard the parable of the sower. In fact, the crowd was so large that Jesus was forced to get into a boat and teach from there (see Matt. 13:2). The throngs of people stood on the shore looking out. All the people heard, but only some of them understood.

Here again we see the subversive nature of the kingdom. Jesus, just like the sower from His story, spread the seed of the kingdom, the word of God. And in the audience on the beach, that seed fell on all different sorts of ground. Everyone heard, but only a few understood. Only a few represented the good soil in the parable. The good soil not only hears but understands and responds.

> **According to the parable, what is the result when the seed falls on the good soil?**

> **Why do you think Jesus gave differing amounts of crop yielded by the good soil?**

When the good seed of the kingdom lands on the good soil of a person's heart, the result is a crop. While the visible results are different on a case-by-case basis, in every case there is fruit.

> **Read Matthew 12:33-37. What is the relationship between a person's words and a person's heart?**

How did Jesus liken that to His illustration of trees and fruit?

The fruit reveals the kind of tree that produces it. If a tree bears apples, then it's an apple tree. If it bears oranges, it's an orange tree. Similarly, a person's life reveals whether or not the seed of the kingdom is growing in his heart.

How would you describe your own heart if it were a type of soil?

What are some daily practices you might more fully commit to in order to make sure your heart is good soil?

To some degree, each of these soils represents our hearts at different times in our lives. There are moments when we are like the hard ground. We hear the good news of the kingdom but choose not to understand. We choose not to follow.

At other times, our hearts are shallow. We get excited initially about the work of the kingdom but then we just stop. Sometimes we stop because our hearts are like the thorny soil. We get so busy that kingdom thought and work is choked out.

We would do well to pray that God would make our hearts into good soil so that we might fully know and embrace His subversive kingdom. Ironically, sometimes our religious tendencies are what most prevent us from hearing and understanding the words of the kingdom. That's how it was in the days of Jesus and how it is today. People caught up in status-quo religion miss out on the kingdom because the kingdom is subversive of the status quo.

With all their attempts to honor God, why do you think the Pharisees missed the kingdom?

Have you ever felt like a Pharisee? When?

sowing for the kingdom

What happens to people whose hearts are good soil? According to the parable, they receive the word of the kingdom. That seed germinates inside them, and eventually it yields a great harvest: "Some 100, some 60, and some 30 times what was sown" (Matt. 13:8). In other words, there is an outward display of what's going on inside of them.

What different forms might that outward display take?

Name some fruit you see in other people's lives.

The kingdom is always growing. It's always moving out. When the seed of the kingdom truly takes root in someone's heart, it's impossible for it to stay hidden. That seed bears fruit. One of the ways it bears fruit is that kingdom people eventually become bearers of the kingdom message themselves.

Read 2 Corinthians 5:20-21. What word did Paul use to describe believers?

Why do you think he chose that word?

List three other words that came to mind when you read the word "ambassador" (v. 20).

1.

2.

3.

When we enter God's kingdom, we become ambassadors of that kingdom on earth. We live and move among the residents of the world's kingdom, sowing seeds of the kingdom of God wherever we go. As we do, we can follow the example of the farmer in the parable of the sower.

How did the farmer in Jesus' story sow the seed?

What can we learn from that?

It's not up to us to choose where the seed grows. Often, the good soil may be where we least expect to find it. And, alternatively, the bad soil might just be where we would expect to find the good. That was certainly the case as Jesus indiscriminately and liberally spoke the word of God.

Looking at His situation, one might expect the best soil to be found among the religious people of the day. They were the ones who had studied the law and dedicated their lives to following it. They seemed to be the most devout, the ones who looked expectantly forward to the coming Messiah. And yet these people's hearts proved to be bad soil when the seed of the kingdom didn't grow inside them.

Think about those who proved to be the good soil. In many cases they were the outcasts, the destitute, the poor, and the downtrodden. They gave themselves fully to Jesus' message of the kingdom of God. Who could have predicted such surprising results? But we can learn from the shock.

> From Jesus' practices, what principles can we learn about the places where the kingdom should be preached?

> What about the ways the gospel should be spread?

> Where are you currently sowing kingdom seeds by sharing the good news of the kingdom?

We aren't responsible for producing the crop. God does a fine job of that on His own. He doesn't need our help. Our job, once the kingdom is implanted in our hearts, is to sow the seed of the kingdom. We are to sow that seed far and wide, in places where we expect it to grow and in places where we don't think such growth is possible.

> When we sow God's word as indiscriminately and liberally as the sower in the story, what are expressing we believe?

Specifically, what does such a commitment communicate about our belief in God?

When we follow the example of the sower, we show that we truly trust the results to God. We sow in faith—not faith in our ability to look and determine what kind of soil a person's heart is, but that maybe God can still make a crop grow in the most unlikely of places.

To truly become sowers of the kingdom, our preferences, expectations, and impulses must be transformed. We have to get over our personal opinions and judgments and be willing to be ambassadors of the kingdom wherever—and to whomever—the Lord chooses to send us.

In your life, what is the biggest obstacle to sowing the seed of the kingdom as generously as the sower in the parable did?

How often do you pray that God would use you to advance His kingdom? Spend some time doing that now.

subversive
kingdom

kingdom extending

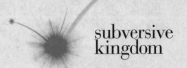
subversive
kingdom

SESSION 3

GETTING STARTED

1. Share one insight or new way of thinking about the parable of the sower based on your study this week.

2. What is the relationship between the parable of the sower and the kingdom of God?

3. Think about another dynamic of the kingdom with your group: opposition. Specifically, what are some ways Satan might actively oppose the kingdom of God?

4. On a scale of 1 to 10, with 1 being inactive and 10 being very active, share how active you believe yourself to be in spiritual warfare. Why did you choose the number you did?

PRESSING IN

Watch the teaching segment from the DVD using the viewer guide below.

Because of our _____ and _____, the world is in rebellion against the rightful rule of God.

Christians are the _____ against the rebellion.

We are in the midst of a spiritual battle with a _____ outcome.

The world is dead, dark, and ruled by the _____.

_____ is active in opposing the work of God.

Christians must _____, but not fear, the work of Satan.

We respond to the spiritual battle by being a _____ _____ for the gospel and the kingdom where we live.

The world is both _____ and _____.

For its lostness, we _____ the good news of Jesus.

For its brokenness, we do ministries of _____.

If we are to represent _____ and His kingdom, we are going to be engaged in ministries of mercy and the proclamation of the gospel.

Discuss the teaching with your group using the questions below.

1. Why is it important to realize that we are in a spiritual battle with a decided outcome?

2. How does doing so change the way you approach challenges in life?

3. Can you recall a particular instance when you encountered the opposition of the Enemy to the advancing of the kingdom? Share that account with your group.

4. Do you think most Christians pay too little or too much attention to Satan? Why is striking balance in the middle important?

5. Think about someone you know who respects, but doesn't fear, the work of Satan. What characteristics about their lives reveal that they walk this balance?

6. This week, your study will focus on the parable of the wheat and the weeds. Do you remember any details from this story? If so, share them with your group.

7. In this parable, Jesus speaks about the Enemy and his efforts to disrupt the kingdom. Describe with your group the general attitude you see in Scripture from Jesus about Satan.

Close with prayer.

LAUNCHING OUT

Scripture Memory

> "Our battle is not against flesh and blood, but against the rulers, against the authorities, against the world powers of this darkness, against the spiritual forces of evil in the heavens." EPHESIANS 6:12

Kingdom Seeking

* Note how many nonbelievers you have a conversation with this week. See if the results surprise you.
* Pray that you would become more aware of the spiritual dynamics happening all around you.
* Write a note to your pastor this week encouraging him as he leads.

Video sessions are available for purchase at *www.lifeway.com/sk*

kingdom extending

Time marched on. The people, once unified under one king, divided into factions, each choosing to live in whatever way most suited them. Often they fell to war among themselves; great rifts of anger and bitterness developed between them. Some scarcely remembered the old life or the old king, but the king remembered his people.

He was a patient ruler—and he had a plan. A lie had destroyed his rule; a lie that took deep root in the hearts of his people. Their hearts would be how he would get them back. The king still had vast resources at his disposal, enough to take back the land by force. But he chose to be more subtle. More strategic. More subversive.

In a wonderfully bold and unexpected move, the king sent his beloved son, the true prince, to live among the people as a common peasant. In doing so, the prince would begin a subversion of his own, a rebellion in the same hearts that had abandoned him and his father long ago. And so the prince began his long journey from his father's house into the unfriendly confines of the land.

For years, he moved inconspicuously through the divided kingdom. He spread the message of his father's kindness and love. People, long deceived by the lies they had believed, started to remember the true nature of the kingdom.

They began to believe again.

But there were some whose hearts had become so wicked that they hated the prince and his message. They did all they could to discredit him and his quiet rebellion. Finally, their anger reached such a fevered pitch that they put the prince to death, causing great sadness among those who had followed him. But the damage had been done. The subversive mission had been successfully launched. Where there had been only one rebel for the king, now there were many. A passion for a new kingdom had been ignited, and people were flocking back to the reign of the true king.

DAY 1 a subversive sower

Jesus lived in an agrarian society, so it shouldn't surprise us that many of His parables use metaphors related to farming. When He told these stories originally, His audience would have resonated with the talk of fields, seed, and crops. These were tangible ideas Jesus used to describe the mysterious and subversive nature of the kingdom.

Read Matthew 13:24-30,36-43. To what does Jesus relate each of the following?

The seed sower:

The field:

The good seed:

The weeds:

One field. Two sowers. One sows good seed and the other sows weeds. As one of the most misunderstood parables in Scripture, the parable of the wheat and the tares has been frequently quoted, misquoted, and misapplied. Fortunately, Jesus explains the meaning of this parable beginning in verse 36.

Look back at Matthew 13:36. To whom did Jesus explain this parable?

What does that indicate about the nature of the kingdom of God?

Here again, Jesus demonstrated that the kingdom of God is mysterious. It's for those who have ears to hear and will remain inscrutable for those who don't. His disciples approached Him in private, and in private Jesus told them about the field of the world, the good seed of the sons of the kingdom, and the two sowers.

The parable begins similarly to the parable of the sower (see Matt. 13:1-9,18-30). God is sowing good seed in a field. But this parable takes a twist. Alongside the good seed, an enemy of the sower came and spread weeds among the wheat.

According to the parable, when did the enemy do his sowing?

What might the fact that the enemy sowed in secret and at night indicate about his character?

What can you surmise about the enemy's intent in sowing?

The landowner in the story did not seem overly concerned that the evil one had sowed weeds among the wheat. When asked by his servants, the landowner merely replied, "Let them grow together until harvest."

Back in real life, Jesus has come, and with Him, the march toward victory for His kingdom has begun. But the kingdom is not yet fully completed. The Enemy hasn't surrendered, and full victory has not been realized. We're still in a great period of tumult. The wheat is still growing: people are coming to Christ, being transformed by the gospel, serving the hurting, and sharing the good news with others.

But, even as the kingdom increases, the Enemy simultaneously sows weeds in the field. We know God is sowing, but there's another force at work too.

The Enemy is working right in the middle of our progress. The field never gets filled with wheat, and weeds continuously spring up as well.

How do the weeds increasing along with the wheat impact the kingdom?

How should our view of the kingdom change in light of the Enemy's efforts?

We can make one of two errors in our perspective on Satan: We may either fail to recognize his existence, or we may put too much stock in his existence. In either case, our focus can be drawn off the progression of the kingdom. If we fail to recognize that the Enemy is constantly sowing weeds in the midst of the good seed, we will constantly be frustrated at the opposition that springs up to the kingdom of God.

On the other hand, we must not give Satan too much credit. Notice another important detail of the parable: The weeds grow in the field by the master's permission. If he wanted to, the landowner could have uprooted the weeds any time, but for the sake of the overall harvest, he allows them to continue to grow until he is ready to harvest the grain.

Satan has a plan. As a part of that plan, he's sowing evil at the same time God is sowing good. It's not one or the other; it's both, sowing at the same time in the same field. Yet we recognize that the true landowner, God Almighty, is far greater than the Enemy. Therefore, we can walk through the field of the world with both awareness and confidence. We are aware the Enemy is at work, but we can be confident in the greater power of God to establish His subversive kingdom.

Which position regarding Satan do you tend to gravitate toward: Never thinking about him at all, or giving him too much credit?

How have you seen the danger in each one?

What are some practical ways you might balance that sense of awareness and confidence?

DAY 2 the expected—and unexpected—results

One field. Two different sowers. Some good seed, and some bad seed. Wheat and weeds. As citizens of the subversive kingdom, we must remember that there are two dynamics working at the same time in the field of the world. Because there are two different sowers, there will be two different results. First of all, there are the expected results.

> **Think back to the parable of the sower that you studied last week. In the end, what characteristic distinguished the true believers from the false ones?**

> **What sorts of things might be characterized as "fruit"?**

> **Why is the production of fruit the defining mark of true belief? What does the presence of fruit indicate?**

It might sometimes be troubling, but often it's impossible to tell who exactly is a true kingdom citizen and who is not, especially when someone first hears and seems to respond positively to the gospel. Though all different types of people might at first receive the good news of Jesus and His kingdom with great joy, only time will tell the depth of that response.

Those who have hearts of good soil will bear fruit of the kingdom. Lives will be changed. The blessing of the gospel will be passed on. True believers will grow in Christlikeness and in their love for the kingdom.

These are the expected results of God's sowing.

> **Read Isaiah 55:8-11. What does God promise in these verses regarding His word?**

> **Rephrase that promise into the language of sowing the good seed.**

> **Given this promise, with what attitude should we sow the seed of the kingdom?**

Just as God provides the rain and sun for seed to grow in any garden, He also causes His word to germinate and grow to fruition in His children's hearts. We can be confident in His good work through the power of His word and the Holy Spirit, and because we are, we can share the good news of the kingdom far and wide without prejudice. But according to the parable, an unexpected result often accompanies God's good work: weeds.

> **Read Matthew 13:26-27. What surprised the landowner's slaves?**

Why did this action of the enemy shock them? Why does it often shock Christians?

The type of weeds referenced in the parable is worthy to note. Specifically, they are called *darnel*. Darnel is a weed that looks just like the wheat. It grows around wheat fields and, in the very early stages of growth, you can't tell the difference between the two. But darnel is poisonous. But because of its nearly identical appearance to wheat, it takes awhile to see what is wheat and what are weeds.

If the weeds are poisonous, what might that poison mean for the kingdom?

Why does it take time to distinguish between the wheat and the weeds?

In this parable, Jesus is the Master and we're the slaves. The reaction of the landowner's slaves is the same as many Christians who have not understood this parable about the kingdom. They are surprised and shocked that people who look like Christians, say they're Christians, and act like Christians in public can be so mean-spirited and angry and act in ways contrary to the gospel in private.

One of the biggest challenges we face is not that people's minds are closed to the gospel. At least you know where those people stand, even if that stance is hostile. But the challenge with weeds in the church is much, much greater.

In the strategy of planting weeds among the wheat, we see the true brilliance of the enemy. Weedlike Christians sow discord and break up community. They see the church as a tool for meeting their personal needs, rather than a means to expand God's kingdom. When something doesn't go their way, weeds are quick to criticize and first in line to throw stones. We've all seen it. Some of us have been on the receiving end of weedy wrath.

But notice that Jesus wasn't surprised by what was going on. Not at all. In fact, He expected it. We, on the other hand, still find it surprising. So what do we do from here?

What are some inappropriate ways to respond to the truth of this parable?

What reaction do you think Jesus is hoping for in His disciples?

How might you move toward such a reaction today?

DAY 3 stay, don't separate

Picking the weeds out seems like a pretty obvious solution to the problem in this parable.

When confronted with the weeds, have you ever wanted to respond as the servants did in Matthew 13:28? Why or why not?

What did the landowner advise his servants to do in Matthew 13:29-30?

Wait. Sometimes that's a hard word to hear from Jesus, and yet waiting is a part of life. When servants want to get rid of the weeds growing amid the wheat, it's frustrating when the landowner instructs them to wait.

When we are surrounded by values and lifestyles that are radically different than those in the kingdom of God, the temptation is to try our best to pull out the weeds. We think to ourselves, *If we could just get rid of the weeds in our community, in our school district, in our government, and in the world, then the kingdom would come in.*

Wrong. If we think we are going to Christianize the world, we are denying the truth that an enemy is sowing seed alongside the wheat. Moreover, great harm comes to the kingdom when we try and uproot worldly weeds.

What is the difference between *evangelizing* the world and *Christianizing* the world?

How might Christianizing the world actually be harmful to the kingdom?

What historical examples can you recall when that has been the case?

A little history here helps us understand what can happen, both when Christians take heed to this parable and when they disregard it. When the church started in the Book of Acts, it was very small. But despite persecution, it grew slowly inside the cities of the Roman Empire, particularly among Jewish people.

Then, in the second and third centuries, a series of plagues rocked the cities. People were sick and dying in mass quantities, and the cities became graveyards. Everywhere people began to flee from the urban environments out of fear. But while most were running away, the Christians chose to stay and care for the sick, poor, hurting, and dying. After that, Christianity truly began to spread rapidly. People entered the kingdom in droves, all because the Christians were willing to stay rather than run.

Who in your life has chosen to "stay" when times were hard for you?

Why do you think staying with the sick and dying was such a catalyst for Christian growth?

The kingdom was spread far and wide. Soon the Roman Empire—once hostile to Christ-followers—came to be a place where the majority of the people were Christian. It was just a matter of time until the emperor officially declared the empire to be "Christian." In fact, the name was eventually changed to "Holy Roman Empire."

At first glance, we might see such a turn as a tremendous victory for the kingdom. This was not the case, however, because those who Christianized the land forgot there were weeds among the wheat.

During the plagues, the children of the kingdom were the obedient servants who waited according to the landowner's instruction. They knew that not all of the sick and dying were wheat, but they didn't try and uproot them. Instead, they loved and cared for them, praying that God, in His miraculous power, would change them from weeds to wheat.

Christians sensed the urgency of the moment. They didn't worry about the conduct of society at large; they concerned themselves with the souls of the dying. If we focus all our attention on the conduct of culture, we do little about the condition of the hearts of those around us.

A Christianized empire is far different from God's kingdom. The temptation is for us to take on the role of separating weeds from wheat that Jesus reserves for Himself. We are not meant to separate the wheat from the weeds in the world. Separation is Jesus' job, and He is very qualified to do it.

Knowing that separation of the weeds from the wheat is Jesus' job, how should Christians respond?

How should such knowledge impact the way that we interact with the world around us?

DAY 4 insiders and outsiders

In the kingdom, we leave the separating to Jesus. We recognize the reality of the weeds as well as the wheat, but we trust Jesus, in His wisdom, that it's best to wait until harvest time to distinguish between them.

Paul's letter to the Corinthian church also emphasized that believers and unbelievers will both occupy this world until it ends.

> Read 1 Corinthians 5:9-10. With whom did Paul say not to associate?

> Read the passage again. Were these immoral people inside or outside the church?

> Why does it matter?

In short, Paul advised, "I told you to not hang around people like that. Don't be like them." But there's another key to his instructions in the following verse. Paul further writes in verse 10:

> "I did not mean the immoral people of this world or the greedy and swindlers or idolaters; otherwise you would have to leave the world."

That's a very important distinction.

Paul says clearly that when he instructed the Corinthians not to associate with immoral people, he did not mean the immoral among unbelievers. It's clear that Paul agrees with Jesus' expectation that the wheat and the weeds will exist together in the world. This fact didn't surprise Jesus. Nor did it shock Paul.

Paul then says that avoiding the immoral among unbelievers would require Christians to literally leave the world. Such an idea was unthinkable to Paul and to Jesus.

> **Read John 17:14-18. What did Jesus mean when He said "the world"?**

How did Jesus pray that the children of the kingdom would relate to the world?

Jesus didn't preach isolationism, that His followers should avoid the world in order to avoid sin. Instead, He specifically said He was sending Christians into the world for the sake of the kingdom. Paul followed a similar line. What Paul says in 1 Corinthians is the same thing Jesus told us in the parable—that as long as life continues on earth Christians and unbelievers will always share the same space. It's unavoidable—and that's not a bad thing.

> **How would our communities and world change if Christians refused to engage unbelievers where they live, work, or play?**

We can't keep ourselves from impure people. It's impossible. We see them every day. At work. At the grocery store. In our neighborhoods. Maybe even in our own families. The thing is, Jesus isn't calling us to avoid them. He didn't tell us to leave this world and seclude ourselves from immoral people. He just said He will do the separating at the end. Him. Not us.

When we look at unbelievers as if they are to be avoided, how does that affect our ability to share Christ with them?

How can you be more intentional about interacting with non-Christians in the world?

Read on in 1 Corinthians 5:11-12. Who was Paul talking about in this passage?

The insiders Paul described here are those in fellowship with the church. And they were the focus of the problem Paul addressed in this passage. Paul was not giving instruction about those in the world, but about those in the church.

What's the difference between an insider acting immorally
and an outsider acting immorally?

Why should it matter to Christians?

It's not our job to judge those outside—that's up to Jesus. Though as believers
we are called to handle the problem of insiders acting like outsiders. Scripture
teaches that when you know an insider is behaving as an outsider, your job is to
do something about it. Continuing in verse 12, Paul says, "Don't you judge those
who are inside?" God judges the outsiders. But you Christians? You put away the
evil person from among yourselves.

Why do you think Jesus told us not to separate the wheat
and the weeds in the world but to separate the wheat and
the weeds in the church?

What happens to the church's reputation when sin in the
membership is overlooked?

Confronting overt sin in the local church is called church discipline. American congregations rarely engage in church discipline. Even though we are biblically commanded to look to one another, provoke one another to love and good deeds, and hold each other accountable, for the most part we do not take this charge seriously. It's one of those Scriptures we say we believe but typically do not obey.

There are many people who live like unbelievers but are in fellowship with the church, though perhaps that fellowship is in name only. They may be on the church membership list. They mistakenly think that if they joined the church at some point, they're OK with God. There even are some church attendees whose lives, privately or publicly, don't reflect the life Jesus calls us to live in His name.

We are to exercise church discipline as we seek to restore any professed brother or sister in Christ who has strayed from the truth and is living in sin. We are called to maintain a biblical community of Christians who hold each other accountable.

But, we must not confuse the standards we're called to uphold in the church with the way we relate to the rest of the world. Wheat and weeds are sown together and are going to grow together. Jesus expects it; so must we.

How involved are you in both being held accountable and holding other people accountable for their actions?

How can you encourage a more active attempt at doing so in your church?

DAY 5 kingdom wheat

The weeds will always grow with the wheat because Satan is sowing in the same field as God. Jesus expected it. We should too. Despite that fact, we can't separate ourselves from the rest of the world and expect to expand the kingdom.

Neither can we separate ourselves from discipline within the kingdom. It's our job to make sure that we hold those who call themselves Christians accountable when they act counter to the character of Christ.

> **As part of Jesus' kingdom, with which of the lessons do you struggle most?**
>
> **a) God and Satan are sowing in the same field.**
>
> **b) Only fruit signifies a Christian life.**
>
> **c) We must live and remain holy among the weeds.**
>
> **d) We must hold accountable other Christians when they act like weeds.**
>
> **Why?**

That's a lot to think about in just a few short verses. But there's a bit more we can glean from this parable. In Matthew 13:30, the master says this:

> "Let both grow together until the harvest. At harvest time I'll tell the reapers: Gather the weeds first and tie them in bundles to burn them, but store the wheat in my barn."

Both the wheat and the weeds are growing together, here and now. This growth will continue until Jesus comes back. And then He'll send His angels to gather up the weeds and throw them to the side to be burned. It might be hard to imagine, but that's what is coming. Among those bundles will be many people who look and act like Christians but have actually been weeds all along.

But the wheat? It will be stored in God's barn, given eternal glory rather than eternal punishment. Judgment is best left in God's hands; it's not our job to do that in the world. Neither is it our job to moralize the unconverted.

Don't miss that crucial point: *It's not our job to moralize the unconverted.* So in the kingdom, what are we supposed to spend our time doing based on the parable of the wheat and the weeds?

We must convert the immoral.

What's the difference between moralizing the unconverted and converting the immoral?

Why must we concentrate our efforts on conversion and not moralizing?

Think about our world in its current state. Consider a scenario in which all acts of terrorism cease. And there is no more adultery. Or murder or violence. Also, no one is oppressed nor goes to bed hungry at night. All are patient, hard working, respectful, and hospitable.

These are all good things, to be sure. But without Jesus, those good things are eternally insufficient. Likewise, life in the kingdom is not limited to polite, well-behaved citizens. We don't want people to just behave morally. We want them to know Jesus. We want a real change of heart, change of life. We want them to come into the kingdom.

And we want them to grow as wheat in the world.

In these days between the time of the inauguration and the consummation of the kingdom, it is our charge to advance the kingdom of God until Jesus comes back to set it up in its fullness.

What's the end result of the battle we, as Christians, are currently fighting?

Is it easy to get confused about which battles we are to fight? Why or why not?

How do we measure success along the way?

If all we do is fight cultural battles, we are doing very little to add people to the kingdom of God. Sure, there are going to be weeds, but God will take care of those in the end. For now—for us—we would do well to focus our energies, efforts, and prayer on converting the weeds of the world rather than plucking them out.

subversive
kingdom

SESSION 4

kingdom hidden

subversive
kingdom

SESSION 4

GETTING STARTED

1. Based on your study this week, what was Jesus' main point in telling the parable of the wheat and the weeds?

2. Did you find yourself more aware of the work of the Enemy because of your study this week? Why or why not?

3. Jesus described the kingdom as being like a mustard seed. With your group list all the ways that the kingdom might be like this small seed.

4. Jesus further described the kingdom as being like yeast. Make another list with your group of the ways that the kingdom might be like yeast.

PRESSING IN

Watch the teaching segment from the DVD using the viewer guide below.

Sometimes we, as Christians, are influenced by the values of the world into thinking that the key to advance the kingdom of God is the "_____."

The kingdom starts _____, spreads in, and changes from the _____ out.

Too often we want a _____ version of the gospel and Christianity in which the church becomes a distributor of religious goods and services.

Christians are not customers but _____ in the gospel.

When governments seek through _____ _____ to restrict the advance of the gospel it actually promotes the advance of the gospel.

When governments through political will seek to advance the gospel it actually _____ the gospel.

Real change takes place in _____ because of the lives changed by the power of the gospel.

We must both be _____ and make a _____.

Discuss the teaching with your group using the questions below.

1. Do you agree that we, in the church, are often preoccupied with the "big"? Why do you think that is?

2. Why do you think Jesus seemed to disperse crowds rather than gather them?

3. Would you consider yourself more of a "church customer" or a "colaborer"? Why?

4. Who are some people in your past who have contributed to the kingdom in seemingly small ways that then grew to be enormous?

5. Have you seen the kingdom of God behave in a similar fashion to yeast, where it transforms something from the inside out?

6. How are you currently involved in both the proclamation of the gospel and the demonstration of the gospel in practical ways? How would you like to be more involved?

Close with prayer.

LAUNCHING OUT

Scripture Memory

"Thanks be to God, who always puts us on display in Christ and through us spreads the aroma of the knowledge of Him in every place." 1 CORINTHIANS 2:14

Kingdom Seeking

* Consider what small ways you might contribute to the kingdom through the ministries of your church.
* Write a note to someone in your life who has encouraged you in small ways. Let them know how meaningful their support has been.
* Spend some time reviewing your Scripture memory verses.

kingdom hidden

The people of the new kingdom talked often about the words of the prince. As they reflected back on their time with him, they realized that he had been teaching them how to live in his father's kingdom in his absence. It was almost as if the prince had known his time with them would be short, and he was seeking to pack his life into theirs.

They stumbled at times, forgetting the nature of the prince and the king, but they held onto the hope that there would come a day when the prince would return. When he did, he would set things right in the whole land again. But until he did, they knew it was their responsibility to live out the nature of the true kingdom in this hostile land. And hostile it was.

There were those in the land who sought to stamp out their rebellion with violence. The attacks were brutal and merciless, but the king's people remained faithful. They had fallen in love with the rule of their rightful king and refused to be dissuaded. Thanks to their perseverance and faith, those who believed in the king grew in wisdom as well as number. They set up outposts all over the land— sanctuaries of the true kingdom inside the hostile territory.

But these outposts served as little more than meeting places for the people. They walked in and among the people of the land, just as they had seen the prince do. In so doing, they were able to spread his message of forgiveness for turning from the king's rule and invite others to remember his goodness.

Once again, the great enemy faced a dilemma. He sensed the tide beginning to turn, and he was not content to lose the chaos and disarray he had worked so hard to instill. But, what to do?

DAY 1 small is good

The kingdom of God is a subversive kingdom. According to the will of God, it moves irresistibly to displace the kingdom of darkness, often operating in surprising and unpublicized ways. For that reason, among others, the kingdom continues to be a mysterious reality and difficult to grasp in the world—even among those who know a thing or two about God.

Take John the Baptist, for example. If ever there was a man who you'd think would fully understand and embrace the kingdom of God, surely it was John.

Are you familiar with the biblical account of John the Baptist? If so, what three things come to mind when you think about him?

1.

2.

3.

Would it surprise you to know that even John misunderstood some things about the mission and kingdom of Jesus? Why or why not?

Read Matthew 11:1-6. Why do you think John had questions about Jesus' identity?

Even before he was born John, the cousin of Jesus, leaped in his mother's womb when Mary, the mother of Jesus, arrived for a family visit (see Luke 1:41). After reaching adulthood and fulfilling his calling as a prophet, John had boldly declared that Jesus was the "Lamb of God, who takes away the sin of the world" (John 1:29). When he baptized Jesus, John had seen the Holy Spirit descend on Jesus as a dove and heard the heavenly endorsement: "This is My beloved Son. I take delight in Him!" (Matt. 3:17).

Despite this background, even John had trouble recognizing the coming kingdom of God. Along with most of his countrymen, John expected a dramatic invasion. Political upheaval, judgment of enemies, and prominence for the people of God were to be signs of the kingdom. In short, they were expecting big. But they instead got small.

Why might Jesus' inauguration of the kingdom be called "small"?

How likely is it that Christians today might miss the kingdom because of its "smallness"? Why?

The kingdom of God showed up when Jesus the king showed up, and yet His advent was in the most surprising and inconspicuous manner imaginable. A king would have been expected to show up in Rome, the political and cultural center of the entire world. Instead, Jesus' birth was born in a small Mediterranean province in the middle of nowhere, a nothing-town called Bethlehem.

The King of kings and Lord of lords used a completely insignificant town to inaugurate His kingdom that would take over the whole world. So when Jesus talked about the small things of the kingdom of God in Matthew 13, we should not be surprised. He modeled that smallness.

Read Matthew 13:31-32. How would you summarize Jesus' main point in this parable?

Read Matthew 13:33. How do you think the parable of the mustard seed relates to the parable of the yeast?

Like the people in Jesus' day, we tend to think that bigger is always better. After all, if something is good, it will catch on. Volume then becomes the sure sign of something good. Big is good because big is successful.

Right?

Wrong—at least in the kingdom of God. Rather than comparing the kingdom to something as massive and expansive as a mountain range or the ocean, Jesus instead opted in these parables to bring out the nature of the kingdom as seen in something as small and seemingly insignificant as a mustard seed and a bit of yeast.

Are you tempted to always look for the biggest and best in Christianity to which you attach yourself? Why or why not?

Why might that be a dangerous attitude?

How do you think you might embrace the "smallness" of the kingdom Jesus talked about in Matthew 13:31-33?

DAY 2 the danger of big

The kingdom of God invades the earth. God ushers in that kingdom by wrapping Himself in human flesh. With Jesus comes a new day of relational intimacy and missional urgency brought upon the world. Those are pretty big things. Then why would Jesus liken such a kingdom not as big but as something very, very small?

That is precisely what He did in Matthew 13:31-32:

> "The kingdom of heaven is like a mustard seed that a man took and sowed in his field. It's the smallest of all the seeds, but when grown, it's taller than the vegetables and becomes a tree, so that the birds of the sky come and nest in its branches."

Record below three questions you have on first reading this parable.

1.

2.

3.

Notice that unlike the previous parables, Jesus gives no interpretation of this parable or the following one about yeast (see v. 33). Why do you think that is?

Jesus literally couldn't have picked anything smaller to liken to the kingdom of God. The mustard seed was the smallest seed known in Palestine at that time. While our American mentality of "bigger is better" might push back on such a comparison, Jesus was unembarrassed, unashamed, and unperturbed in saying that the kingdom has such a humble beginning.

Read another reference to the mustard seed in
Matthew 17:20. What was Jesus saying about the
nature of faith in this passage?

Bigger does not always mean better, either in the case of faith or the kingdom.
As counterintuitive as it might seem, the small is actually the most effective way
for the kingdom to be advanced, even in our day.

Throughout Christian history, the desire to be "big" has diluted the message
of the gospel and gotten the church into trouble. Christianity thrived when it
was an underground movement, persecuted by governments and threatened by
communities. When the movement of the kingdom became big with the Roman
Empire's legalization of Christianity, soon to follow were corruption, materialism,
and half-hearted worship.

In what modern examples is the same tendency visible?

What do you think are some of the dangers of being big?

The same dynamic is clearly visible in the world today. In the United States, we have enormous churches and a majority population who claims the name of Jesus, yet North America is the only continent in the world where the church is not growing.

Every day in the United States eight churches close their doors—that's more than 50 a week! By contrast, in a country like China in which the government is constantly trying to clamp down on Christianity, a great movement of God is happening. There are between 50 and 80 million Christians gathering together consistently, most of them in small house churches proclaiming the gospel and exploding in growth.[1]

Perhaps that's because in North America, we've fallen in love with being big rather than with Jesus and the gospel. If bigger is better, then it seems our churches should be doing great, right? This is not always the case, as being big carries its own challenges.

One of these dangers is that bigness can turn Christians into *consumers*. By consumers we don't refer simply to people who buy things, but to those who take *from* ministry and never *contribute to* ministry. In large churches, there is the temptation for Christians to sit and watch the show. After a while if "the show" no longer holds their interest, they become disgruntled. This was not what they paid for!

The result is that we often see large churches "swapping sheep," as bored consumers move from one show to the next.

While it can be a challenge for larger churches to involve the majority of their members in ministry, smaller churches, at least in theory, should be able to involve a greater percentage of people. In smaller churches organizing ministry should be easier and accountability should be more readily at hand. For flexibility and quick response time, small is the new big!

No, small isn't bad. Small is good. That does not mean we necessarily strive for smaller, rather than bigger, but we will do well to think and act small, even when we are large.

Do you more often come to church as a consumer or a contributor? Why?

What are some practical ways you might be a more active participant in small advances of the kingdom of God?

DAY 3 good growth

On reading the parable of the mustard seed, we might first conclude that Jesus is against big. That He doesn't like or want big ministries, big impact, or big goals. That's only partly true because the mustard seed and the kingdom both begin in the small, but there is a tremendous amount of growth that then takes place. As surprising as the initial size of the seed is, it's perhaps even more surprising when that tiny seed produces a tree "taller than the vegetables … so that the birds of the sky come and nest in its branches" (Matt. 13:32).

If Jesus isn't against the kingdom growing big, why is it important to appreciate the smallness of its beginning?

What principles about kingdom growth can you identify based on this comparison with the mustard seed?

We might easily get caught up in the details of the parable at this point. What are the vegetables? What are the birds? What's the sky? What's the nest? What are the branches? However in interpreting these kingdom parables, we must remember that parables aren't supposed to be seen as allegories—not every detail has a specific meaning. When we look for the overarching theme, it is clear that the point is the surprising result of the kingdom's growth. From the smallest of seeds comes a shockingly large mustard bush that's as big as a tree. So big in fact, the birds have a place to rest in its branches.

How big is that in terms of the kingdom? Very big, in fact.

Read Psalm 72:8 and Revelation 11:15. According to these verses, how big will the kingdom of God grow?

Thinking back to the growth of the mustard plant, how will that growth happen?

It's likely that Jesus had in His mind the Old Testament prophecy from the Book of Ezekiel in which the tree, representative of Israel, would grow and become mighty. Read Ezekiel 17:23:

> "I will plant it on Israel's high mountain
> so that it may bear branches, produce fruit,
> and become a majestic cedar.
> Birds of every kind will nest under it,
> taking shelter in the shade of its branches."

There will come a time when the kingdom rules over all. That's pretty large, and yet we have to be careful. When we see these pictures painted by Scripture, we might be tempted to think that the kingdom is destined to take over the whole world through human effort. Some throughout history have taken that to mean the goal of believers should be to Christianize the world. The problem in that sort of thinking is that it fails to account for one of the key truths of the parable of the wheat and the weeds—namely, that Satan constantly sows weeds in with the wheat.

If the kingdom of God is subversive, what are some signs
of its growth?

Is that how Christians typically think about growth? If not,
what are the differences?

We've already recounted when the Roman emperor Constantine declared Rome
to be Christianized. The Roman Empire eventually became the Holy Roman
Empire. The entirety of Europe was recognized as Christendom. But today, when
we go to Europe, we don't see a Christian country or a Christian worldview. Much
of that former empire is remarkably unchurched and filled with people who are
not followers of Christ.

The answer then is not to Christianize the governments, institutions, and ruling
kingdoms of the world and expect individuals to fall in line. Instead, we see from
the mustard plant that good growth happens below the surface long before the
above-ground evidence.

Do you agree with the previous statement? What does it
mean that growth happens below the surface?

What is the benefit when growth happens below the surface
before it explodes above the surface?

The kingdom of God is subversive. It spreads out like the mustard seed's
expanding root system, just below the surface, moving quietly among the
people, right under the noses of supervising institutions. Then when you least
expect it, the true growth at last becomes visible. In all of that "silence" the
kingdom has been spreading through little ways, slowly but surely becoming big.

How does this fact change your perspective on kingdom
growth?

What are a few ways you might be more in touch with the
often subversive growth of the kingdom of God?

DAY 4 permeation

The small seed of the kingdom grows and spreads below the surface and eventually becomes plainly visible above. In the parable of the yeast, Jesus described the nature of this subversive growth.

Read Matthew 13:33. What do you think is the main point of this parable?

How do you think the way yeast works relates to the kingdom of God?

What other times can you recall that yeast is mentioned in the Bible? What did it symbolize?

Yeast in the Bible is sometimes symbolic of sinful things. Take, for example, the words of Jesus in Luke 12:1:

"Be on your guard against the yeast of the Pharisees, which is hypocrisy."

In this passage, the yeast is directly representative of hypocrisy whereas in Matthew 13 Jesus applied it to the kingdom. But to truly understand either teaching, we've got to have some basic understanding of what yeast does.

Yeast is a substance that reacts with moisture, heat, acidity, or some other trigger to produce gas that becomes trapped inside dough as bubbles. Those bubbles are what cause the dough to rise. Then when the dough is baked, the holes left by the gas bubbles remain, giving breads, cakes, and other baked goods their soft, airy—and delicious, I might add—textures.

> **How does this information help your understanding of Jesus' words?**

> **In looking at both the above passages from Luke 12 and Matthew 13, how does the yeast function in each case?**

There's another interesting detail in this passage that adds to our understanding of the relationship between yeast and the kingdom. In the parable, the yeast is mixed into the dough. The word for *mixed* here can also be translated *hidden*. The yeast is hidden in the flour. Once again, Jesus pointed back to the subversive nature of the kingdom. Just as yeast is hidden inside the dough and begins to quietly do its work from the inside out, so the kingdom is enfolded into all the societies and peoples of the world and slowly, methodically begins to permeate every nook and crevice.

Whether referring to the hypocrisy of the Pharisees or the kingdom of God, yeast is a permeating agent. Hypocrisy was the yeast of the Pharisees. And like yeast, everything they did was tainted with that hypocrisy. It permeated every inch of their being because like yeast, once released, it was impossible to contain.

In what way does the kingdom of God permeate the world around it?

Think about a person in your life who seems to influence every situation in which they find themselves for good. Describe that person below.

The funny thing about yeast is that when left in an environment of dough, it actually becomes so entrenched—*hidden*—inside it, that it changes the very composition of the dough. With yeast, you can have a wonderful basket of bread rolls with dinner. Do you know what you have without yeast? A cracker.

The dough is completely transformed from the inside out. Yeast isn't flashy. It's not overt. It works in the small areas, but it does its job with such relentless consistency that in the end the entire mound of dough has been transformed.

What a perfect way to describe the kingdom of God! This kingdom, which was inaugurated with such an inauspicious beginning, has been working on the inside of people, communities, and entire nations for two thousand years. And over time, we have borne witness to the transformation that can happen when a passion for the kingdom is unleashed in the hearts of God's people.

The yeast is something small that permeates then becomes big. It impacts everything around it. So must we. We must permeate into the home. The workplace. The little league complex. The subdivision. The classroom. Everything.

In which areas of your life have you failed to permeate the kingdom?

Pick one of those areas. How might you be more intentional about doing so in that particular area? Pray about it now.

DAY 5 the scent of Jesus

"The kingdom of heaven is like a mustard seed" (Matt. 13:31).

It begins in the small things.

"The kingdom of heaven is like yeast" (Matt 13:33).

It permeates everything.

We seem to have forgotten both of these truths. We believe that to truly engage in the kingdom work of Jesus Christ we need to immediately have some highly visible, numerically significant, widely recognized impact. That is simply not true. Expanding the kingdom of heaven takes place in the small.

If you want to join Jesus in His kingdom mission, then you have to be involved in the small. In your involvement in the small, you'll be a part of His kingdom agenda to plant the mustard seed that will grow to surprising heights.

What is the small means of involvement for you? Is it teaching a children's Sunday School class? Is it beginning a relationship with a family on your street? Is it eating lunch with a coworker instead of at your desk? Is it volunteering to do the job at the church that no one else wants to do? Is it committing to pray for a different country of the world each day? These may seem like small things, but these are the mustard seeds about which Jesus taught.

Which of the above things resonate with you? Why?

Write your commitment below to join Jesus in the small.

What do you think will be the biggest obstacle to persevering in this area of service?

How might you be proactive in preparing yourself for such an obstacle?

Engaging in the small, and staying with it, is difficult simply because of the lack of recognition and notoriety. There are millions of Christians throughout history whose stories have never been and will never be told. They are the nameless obedient who followed the example of Jesus and did not seek after the limelight. Instead, they valued the kingdom over anything else. No one recognized them. No one knew their names. In many cases, no one may have even realized what kind of mustard sized seeds they were planting. But these are precisely the people who have had a tremendous impact in the subversive kingdom.

Who led Billy Graham to Christ? Or George Whitefield, John Wesley, and Charles Spurgeon? Who shared the gospel with them? Who was the first missionary to bring the gospel among the Maasai people, where a revival broke out that lasted for years? Most, if not all of those people, are unknown. They were doing a mustard seed work that bloomed into a giant shrub. We know the results but not the person.

Think of a person in your life who lived out these principles. What part of his or her life do you find most admirable?

Those small things are good, tangible ways that we see the kingdom spread like yeast. It spreads below the surface, permeating every conceivable area of our lives, communities, and world. But here might be the simplest and most difficult lesson from the parable of the yeast: It implies that we cannot live in some kind of Christianized bubble or create a Christian subculture.

We are called to go out. We are called to permeate the society and culture around us and proclaim the good news. Doing so will mean a drastic and conscious lifestyle alteration for many Christians. We listen to Christian music. We consult Christian experts on parenting. We read Christian books for entertainment. We drink milk from the Christian cow.

If we insist on keeping the kingdom in a safe, little bubble, then the end result will be that nobody far from Christ will ever be closer to Him. When all the yeast is in the jar, the dough will never get a chance to rise.

Read Luke 5:27-30. Why were the Pharisees upset with Jesus?

Looking honestly at your life, would anyone be able to accuse you of the same thing?

What are some ways you might reorder your daily schedule to come in more frequent contact with the lost?

It's much easier to stay in the jar—in the friendly confines of our churches. We like to be together with people who share our values and morals. But if we want to be yeast in the dough, we have to break out and be accused of the same thing the Pharisees accused Jesus of: associating with sinners.

Read 2 Corinthians 2:14. How does God put "us on display"?

What do you think it means that through us, God spreads "the aroma of the knowledge of Him"?

We're to spread the aroma of knowing Jesus throughout our neighborhoods. You know how you can tell if a person is living for the kingdom? It's not that a person's friends and neighbors see him go to church on Sunday. It's that those friends and neighbors are loved and served. That's how a neighborhood is permeated.

Have you permeated your workplace? Have you permeated your family? It might seem small, but the small has a way of growing. Just like mustard seeds. Just like yeast.

1. "The Role of Christianity in China," *American Enterprise Institute for Public Policy Research* [online, cited 1 August 2011]. Available from the Internet: *www.aei.org/site-pages/tocqueville-on-china/ii-the-role-of-christianity-in-china.html*

subversive
kingdom

SESSION 5
kingdom of
sacrifice

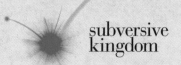

SESSION 5:

GETTING STARTED

1. During your study this week, did the Lord bring to your mind a seemingly small way to contribute to the kingdom? Share it with your group.

2. What was most encouraging to you about the parables of the mustard seed and the yeast? Why?

3. Think about the kind of sacrifices that have to be made in order to extend the kingdom. Who, in your life, has made sacrifices in order to see you grow as a Christian?

4. Do you often think about the sacrifice and cost of being a disciple? Why or why not?

PRESSING IN

Watch the teaching segment from the DVD using the viewer guide below.

To the world, the kingdom of God is _____.

Happiness is _____.

Joy _____ circumstance.

We have an _____ sense of joy because we serve a good, holy, and sovereign King.

Seeking first the kingdom involves _____.

The announcement of the kingdom of God will _____ something.

When we understand the kingdom, we understand the _____ of the kingdom.

The gospel is the good news that God, who is more _____ than we can imagine, looked upon with compassion people, who are more _____ than we would possibly admit, and He sent Jesus into history to establish His kingdom and reconcile people and the world to Himself.

Jesus, whose _____ is more extravagant than we can measure, came to sacrificially die for us, so that we might, by His death and resurrection and through His grace, take hold of new and eternal _____.

Discuss the teaching with your group using the questions below.

1. Do you think the people in the parables focused on the cost they had to pay? Why or why not?

2. Do you think we are more prone to focus on the cost of the kingdom or the joy of the kingdom? Why?

3. Specifically, what do you think fully seeking the kingdom might cost you?

4. Why do you think some Christians fail to see the kingdom as being worth the cost?

5. What is the difference between joy and happiness? Why is it important to understand that distinction?

6. Is there anything unique about the joy of the kingdom? What might be some of the unique attributes of that kind of joy?

7. Think back to the gospel definition given in the teaching session. Which specific part of that definition is the most meaningful to you right now? Why?

Close with prayer.

LAUNCHING OUT

Scripture Memory

> "If anyone wants to come with Me, he must deny himself, take up his cross daily, and follow Me. For whoever wants to save his life will lose it, but whoever loses his life because of Me will save it." LUKE 9:23-24

Kingdom Seeking

* Spend some time on a Web site like that of *The Voice of the Martyrs* (*persecution.org*). Read a few stories about the great sacrifices being made around the world for the kingdom.
* Pray specifically for the persecuted church around the world.
* What is one, tangible area in which you believe God is calling you to sacrifice for the kingdom? Finances? Time? Plans? Make a concrete plan of how to do so.

Video sessions are available for purchase at *www.lifeway.com/sk*

kingdom sacrifice

The enemy knew his own strengths and weaknesses. He had never been one for open warfare, choosing instead to fight his battles behind the scenes, whenever possible. His methods had worked for years in the land; perhaps there was a way they might work again. If there was some way to distract these rebels ...

And just like that, the enemy knew what he would do. His attack would come from within the fledgling tribes rather than outside of them. The tactic would be simple: Divert their focus from the work the prince gave them to do.

The prince left instructions for the kingdom people—share the good news of the true kingdom far and wide. Spread the knowledge of the coming return of the king with all who would listen. If that result was their goal, the great enemy would employ any means necessary to at least slow their progress in achieving it. So the enemy began his efforts to change the focus of the communities.

Shrewdly, he took different and specialized means with each of them. In some cases, he worked through his propaganda to greatly increase the wealth of the believing community. He increased their standard of living so much that they lived in fear of losing what they had gained. The passion they should have had for the kingdom became distorted into a burning desire to protect all they had accumulated. In other outposts, he spread the rumor of attack from the outside, slowly turning the people of the kingdom in on themselves. They built walls around their communities, sequestering themselves from the rest of the land. In still other outposts, the enemy worked to breed hostility toward the culture of the land, convincing the believing people that the best thing for them to do was to attack outsiders.

In each of these cases, the enemy met with success. Many of the kingdom people slowly drifted away from the teachings of their prince. And yet ... yet something troubled him. No matter how hard he tried, no matter how much apparent success he seemed to achieve, there remained a remnant of simple, humble people who spoke quietly and with great faith. Time and time again they pointed the people of the land back to the prince and the true kingdom.

The enemy was greatly frustrated.

DAY 1 "X" marks the spot

It would be any kid's dream. You are walking in a vacant field, one that you've probably been in countless times before, when suddenly your foot strikes something odd. You bend down and brush the dirt off. The wind and weather already did part of the work for you—that must have been why you hadn't seen it before.

So you brush away the rest of the dirt, then pretty soon you find yourself digging a hole with your hands. After several minutes of flying mud and cracked fingernails, you stand up and look down at a chest. Buried treasure! Everyone else missed it, but you found it. And now it's yours!

When you were a kid where did you search for treasure?

What's the closest you've ever come to finding "buried treasure"?

What does it feel like to make such a discovery?

Read Matthew 13:44-46. List below the traits these two parables have in common.

Two stories. Two people. Two objects of great value that were hidden. Then two dramatic responses. Much like the parable of the mustard seed and the parable of the yeast, these are twin parables. Both stories begin with finding something—a buried treasure and a priceless pearl.

But it's the buried treasure that's of particular interest initially, for that treasure illustrates once again a key attribute of the kingdom of God—it's hidden.

Think back over the course of this study so far. In what sense is the kingdom of God a hidden kingdom?

In what sense is it a subversive kingdom?

Remember that the Bible records a significant transition in the teaching ministry of Jesus between Matthew 12 and 13. Before this transition, Jesus spoke openly about the kingdom. He invited people into the kingdom. Following the transition, Jesus began speaking in parables. At first He was willing to explain these stories to His disciples, but by the time He got around to these twin parables, He wasn't explaining any of His stories to anyone. The kingdom was known and public but not any more. Jesus unapologetically says that the kingdom is like a hidden treasure—a secret kingdom.

That doesn't mean it's not there. It doesn't mean it's not accessible. It does mean, however, that it's often found in unlikely places and that there are certain aspects of the kingdom that can be confusing.

Read Luke 10:21. How does this verse relate to the parable of the hidden treasure?

Read 1 Corinthians 2:14. According to this verse, what keeps people from recognizing the kingdom?

How have you seen this dynamic played out in the world?

The kingdom lives in and among the world, and yet it is drastically different from its surroundings. The problem is that somewhere along the line, the people of the kingdom adopted the same values as those around them. There are many Christians out there who fail to see the kingdom as valuable enough to alter their goals in life. Consequently, they set their sights on the same "American dream" of living in a comfortable setting, in close proximity to people with the same skin color or values, and with a nice picket fence separating them from the rest of the world.

If that's the way we choose to live, then we are missing the hidden nature of the kingdom of God. The world's values are not Jesus' values. In the kingdom, Jesus has called us to transfer our allegiance to goals the outside world would look at as utterly insane.

If we began taking a hard look at our lives, what would we see? Would we see that the only difference in our lifestyle and values is the fact that we go to a church service on Sunday? Or would we see something so dramatically different that it attracts confused looks from the people around us?

That's life in the kingdom. The hidden kingdom.

How does your life measure up? Think about the values and goals you have in the following areas. How closely do they align with the goals of the world around you?

Family:

Relationships:

Work:

Finances:

DAY 2 the proper response

The kingdom of heaven is a hidden kingdom, one whose values and priorities are inscrutable to the outside looking in. In this way, it's like a treasure—a hidden treasure. But upon finding that treasure, the man in the parable instantly recognized the great value he had discovered in the field. Without a second thought, he took the drastic action of selling everything he had to buy the field.

Likewise, when the pearl merchant at last found that one, beautiful pearl, he sold everything he had in order to get it. Whether the treasure in the field or the priceless pearl, the response was the same: Each man was willing to give up everything in order to acquire it.

> **Does that reaction seem extreme to you? Why or why not?**

> **If Jesus were to explain how this particular reaction of those in the parables relates to the kingdom, what would you expect Him to say?**

These men, upon finding items of great worth, held nothing back. They willingly sold everything they had because they absolutely had to have this treasure. They sold it all. That part of the subversive kingdom is very, very uncomfortable for us. Much as we hate to admit it, the kingdom of heaven costs us everything.

> **Do you think often about the costliness of the kingdom? Why or why not?**

Have you ever had to give up something in order to pursue Jesus? What were the circumstances?

How have you had the same attitude as these men? Different?

You cannot avoid the simple truth of these parables. If you want to be a part of the kingdom, it's going to cost you. *Everything*. Jesus alluded to this fact, among other places, in Luke 9:23:

> "If anyone wants to come with Me, he must deny himself, take up his cross daily, and follow Me."

What do you think Jesus meant by "take up his cross"?

"Take up your cross" is a phrase that's often quoted but rarely with the gravity it warrants. In Jesus' day, if a person was seen carrying a cross through the middle of a town, there was no doubt that death awaited that person. Public execution to be specific. When Jesus places this demand on His followers, He was requiring nothing short of their entire lives. "Follow Me," Jesus says, "but it's going to cost you everything."

In a practical way, that's the exact demand He laid at the feet of the rich young ruler.

Read Matthew 19:16-22. Why did the young man approach Jesus?

What was Jesus' response? How does Jesus' response relate to the parables of the hidden treasure and the priceless pearl?

How did the young man respond? Why?

The finders of the treasure and the pearl could very well have reacted to their discoveries like the rich young ruler responded to Jesus. This man wanted what Jesus had to offer, but he was not willing to pay the price—to surrender everything. In the end, his possessions were worth more to him than the offer of the kingdom. The men in the parables also might have looked at the box and the pearl as too costly. They might have debated in their minds how much the treasure was worth and what it would cost them to possess something so wonderful. They might have simply kicked dirt back on top of the box or walked away from the pearl shop window.

Unlike the rich young ruler, however, they did not walk away from their treasures. They counted the cost, embraced it, and sold everything they had. In doing so, they remind us of the costly nature of the hidden kingdom. It costs us everything—even intangible things we hold so dear.

The kingdom requires our possessions, true enough. But it also requires our hopes, dreams, preferences, priorities, and families. Nothing is held back in this kingdom. Everything must be given over. That's the only acceptable response.

> **How would you have responded if you were in the place of the rich young ruler?**

> **Is there anything in your life that you're holding back from its kingdom purpose? Spend time praying that God would reveal those things to you and offer them up to Him in response.**

DAY 3 selling with joy

> " 'If you want to be perfect,' Jesus said to him, 'go, sell your belongings and give to the poor, and you will have treasure in heaven. Then come, follow Me.' When the young man heard that command, he went away grieving, because he had many possessions" (Matt. 19:21-22).

What a contrast from the parables of Matthew 13, despite the fact that they have much in common. The parables each involve a person who is seeking, all of whom find something very valuable. But in the case of the rich young ruler, he chose to rebury the hidden treasure or walk away from the pearl of great price. He went away sad because the cost was too great for him to bear.

Look back at Matthew 13:44-46. What motivated the people in these stories to sell everything they had?

What do you think their attitudes were when they began to sell their possessions?

It's interesting that these parables do not indicate either person took a long time to make the decision. They didn't deliberate and brood, thinking intensely about whether it was worth it or not. There was no consideration given to long-term planning, the effect of liquidating their portfolios, or even what their families and friends might think. Instead, the only glimpse into their thinking is provided with just one word: joy.

Think back to a time when you had to give up something for the sake of Jesus or His kingdom. Did you do so with joy? Why or why not?

Do you think most Christians look at sacrifice with an attitude of joy? If not, how do they view sacrifice?

Read Hebrews 12:1-2. What was Jesus' motivation for His great sacrifice?

Perhaps even more surprising than the principle of cost in these parables is the attitude with which the characters embraced that cost. Joy! They followed the example of Jesus, who willingly sacrificed His own life for the sake of the kingdom and yet was motivated by joy.

That's a far cry from the attitude with which we generally view sacrifice. The kingdom costs us everything, but according to these stories, it's a price that we should gladly—even joyfully—pay. Instead of reluctantly forking over our posses-sions, dreams, and aspirations, we immediately slide them across the table to God, without giving it a second thought.

But that's not reality—at least not our reality.

We are much more like the rich young ruler. We like the idea of the kingdom yet are very sad in the end because we can't help but wonder if it's really worth it. In many of our lives, the joy of paying the price is missing.

Do you agree with that last statement? Why or why not?

Why do you think many Christians look with reluctance at sacrificing for the kingdom?

Part of the reason why we fail to have that kind of joy is that we have divided the Christian faith into two experiences. The first experience is the moment we "get saved"; the second is when we die and go to heaven. If that's all life in the kingdom is about, then it makes very little sense to give up all the stuff we might accumulate in the five or so decades in between. But that's not the nature of the gospel.

The gospel is more than just the means by which we are saved. The gospel is the good news that God, who is holier than we can imagine, looked with compassion upon humanity, who is more sinful than we would possibly admit, and sent Jesus into history to establish His kingdom and reconcile people and the world to Himself.

Jesus, whose love is more extravagant than we can fathom, came to sacrificially die for us so we might gain what the Bible defines as eternal life: to know the only true God and take hold of this present life by direction and abundant strength afforded to us by the Holy Spirit.

Is that how you see the gospel? Or is it a burden that keeps you from doing the things you want to do? Does it take away 10 percent of your income and eat away at your Sundays? The gospel is bigger than that. Until we realize it, we might be willing to make a sacrifice for the kingdom, but we'll never do so with joy.

How closely does your view of the gospel match the definition above? In the space below, record the areas in which you would like to grow in that definition.

Write a prayer about those specific areas, asking God to help you see the gospel as bigger.

DAY 4 the worth of the kingdom

The word must have spread through the town like wildfire.

"Did you hear about Joe? He's carrying the stuff out of his house."

"What's he going to do with it?"

"He's selling it to anybody who's walking by!"

The neighbors must have gossiped about financial problems or gambling debts. And imagine their surprise when they heard that he had sold everything—even the home itself—and used the money to buy some worthless field.

Despite the comments about his bizarre behavior, a sly smile must have spread across the seller's face. Joe was well aware of what he was doing, and the whispering didn't bother him at all. He was convinced that what was in that field was worth more than anything and everything else he had.

So is the kingdom of heaven.

> **Read Philippians 3:2-6. What does it mean to "put confidence in the flesh"?**

> **In this passage, how did Paul say he put confidence in the flesh? List all the reasons.**

What would it mean for you to put confidence in the flesh?

The list in these verses was a resume of sorts for someone like Paul. In his culture, all the things listed here would have given him standing in his community and, in his belief system, before God. They were his sources of pride and merit. And yet once he met Jesus, his attitude toward such things changed dramatically.

> Read Philippians 3:7-9. How did Paul's attitude change in regard to those things he formerly thought were so important?

> What was the catalyst for such a dramatic change?

Paul was like a merchant in search of fine pearls. Like a man searching for hidden treasure. When he found the kingdom of heaven, he looked down at those things he once regarded with such high esteem and found them completely lacking in comparison. The value of what he found in Christ tarnished his opinion of all those things he once thought so valuable.

Surely there were people, much like the townspeople above, who looked at Paul as a fool. He was forsaking everything they considered valuable. He was giving away his reputation, his importance, and his marks of prominence. But from Paul's perspective, there was no comparison. He never looked longingly back at what he'd given up because what he gained was worth far more.

> Read Luke 9:23-24. Was Jesus' focus in this verse on losing or gaining? Support your answer based on the verse.

Jesus knew the worth of the kingdom. He also knew it costs everything to really find the kingdom. His focus in this verse wasn't on the loss, however, but on the gain. He knew the pathway to gain went through loss.

Specifically, it's the "surpassing value of knowing Christ Jesus my Lord" (Phil. 3:8) that drove Paul. For Paul, the kingdom was not about going to church. It wasn't about grudging obedience. It certainly wasn't about keeping a list of do's and don'ts. It was about gaining Christ, the greatest treasure in the world.

> Read John 17:3. How did Jesus define eternal life in this passage?

> Do you think about eternal life in those terms?
> Why or why not?

Do you think Paul did? How do you know?

The kingdom life is characterized by the great worth of knowing Jesus. That's what He bought for us on the cross. When we begin to see the surpassing greatness of knowing Christ, we start to see that the cost is minimal when compared to what we gain.

If you have a personal relationship with Jesus Christ, when was the last time you had a personal conversation with Him?

What is standing in your way of developing that relationship?

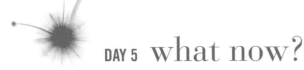

We would be hard-pressed to find a more vivid description of the infinite worth of the kingdom and a more drastic response than what we see in the twin parables of the hidden treasure and the priceless pearl. These stories illustrate that the hidden kingdom of God is of such great value that those who clearly see it completely dedicate themselves to it, not with reluctance but with joy.

> Read these parables once more in Matthew 13:44-46.
> In what way are you most like the people represented there?

> In what way are you least like them?

The problem is that very few of us live in the midst of such a reality. Life in the kingdom, according to our experience, isn't so much characterized by joy as by drudgery. Not by delight, but by obligation. We cling to our possessions, dreams, and goals with white knuckles and only give them up for the sake of the kingdom with tears in our eyes and bitterness in our hearts.

That doesn't seem like finding a great treasure or a priceless pearl.

> Read Ephesians 1:15-19. Record below specifically what
> Paul prayed for the Ephesian Christians.

Which part of his prayer is most applicable to you, given how you relate to the parables in Matthew 13?

At first glance, this prayer might not make sense to us. Remember, the original readers of this letter weren't unbelievers; they were Christians. Despite that, Paul prayed that "the perception of your mind may be enlightened so you may know what is the hope of His calling" (Eph. 1:18).

It seems that some of the Ephesians were in the same state in which many Christians today find themselves—with a misunderstanding of the gospel. We might read the words of Matthew 13 and say, "I can understand how finding a treasure would be transforming. I can understand how finding such a pearl would be exciting. But that's not how I understand the gospel."

A gospel that doesn't inspire joy and doesn't call us to give everything up for the sake of Jesus is a shallow, incomplete—perhaps even false—gospel.

Do you agree with that last statement? Why or why not?

If that statement is true, then how might we begin to embrace the true gospel that calls us to joyful sacrifice?

There is great joy in the promise of heaven, but the gospel goes well beyond that promise. Right here and right now, Christians live in the riches of His inheritance among the saints. When we begin to see the extent of how rich we already are in Christ, the call to sell everything becomes much less consequential. We gladly do so because it's like trading rags for riches.

There are some practical things we can do to nurture a greater understanding of the gospel. For example, we might begin to wean ourselves off the things of this world. All our efforts to make ourselves comfortable actually only serve the purpose of dulling our senses to what true riches are. Like someone who has gotten used to eating only candy bars every day, we no longer have an appreciation for fine food, though its quality is far better. By taking active steps to remove our materialistic, American-dream-chasing tendencies, we will find our spiritual senses heightened.

What are three ways you might heighten your spiritual senses by removing materialistic comforts?

1.

2.

3.

Ultimately, only a work of the Holy Spirit helps us see the kingdom for the treasure it is. It's a matter of prayer, just as it was for Paul and the church at Ephesus. We need to actively be praying over own lives with Paul's prayer for the Ephesians, that the eyes of our hearts would be enlightened to see just how great is our inheritance in Christ. Slowly but surely, we will find ourselves waking up to the immense value of the hidden, subversive kingdom.

subversive
kingdom

kingdom rewards

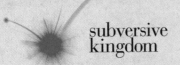

SESSION 6

GETTING STARTED

1. Think back over the course of your study of the subversive kingdom. What one truth has impacted you most? Why?

2. What is one specific way you think the Lord has changed you as a result of your study?

3. Now consider one of the first questions you answered. How important is it that you have a good understanding of the nature of the kingdom of God? Why?

4. How would you respond if someone asked you, "What is the kingdom of God?"

PRESSING IN

Watch the teaching segment from the DVD using the viewer guide below.

"I choose, for one, to meet Him face to face, no faithless servant frightened from my task, but ready when the Lord of the harvest calls; and therefore, with all reverence, I would say, 'Let God do His work, we will do ours.' Bring in the candles."

We are waiting _____ and _____ between the times.

God has placed us here to do _____ _____ in light of His soon and coming return.

We are to wait actively, responsibly, and _____ in light of eternity.

There are kingdom _____ coming based on how we live.

We are _____ waiting in light of the return of our Master.

All are called to be _____ of the kingdom.

We minister in _____ and in _____ using our gifts.

Churches become _____ of the kingdom of God where their agenda is to do the work of the King of kings and the Lord of lords.

Discuss the teaching with your group using the questions below.

1. What are you waiting for in life right now?

2. Has the waiting changed you? How?

3. As Christians, what are some of the right ways we might wait for the return of Jesus?

4. Why is it important to do so?

5. Do you think most Christians consider the eternal rewards waiting for the faithful? Why or why not?

6. What are some practical ways your everyday life would change if you began to see yourself as a steward?

7. How has this study of God's subversive kingdom impacted the way you want to live?

8. What about your church? What specifically are you praying for your church in light of your study?

Close with prayer.

LAUNCHING OUT

Scripture Memory

"We are His creation, created in Christ Jesus for good works, which God prepared ahead of time so that we should walk in them." EPHESIANS 2:10

Kingdom Seeking

※ Share with someone who was not a part of your study a few things God has taught you over the past several weeks about His subversive kingdom.
※ Record in your journal some specific ways that you might be involved in the growth and expansion of the kingdom of God.
※ Consider leading another Bible study group through *Subversive Kingdom.*

Video sessions are available for purchase at *www.lifeway.com/sk*

kingdom rewards

The king watched with great joy as the people woke up to the realities of his goodness and love. He longed for the day when he would return to his people and again walk freely among them, recognized far and wide as the true ruler of the land.

The kingdom people in the land shared his longing. They talked often of the king, knowing that though he might seem absent, his return was imminent. Any day they might look to the horizon and see his advancing army preceding him. What a wonderful day that would be!

As they waited with great expectancy, they began to feel more and more that the land in which they now lived was not their true home—or at least not the way their true home should be. They lived and worked like any other citizens, and yet in their hearts they were profoundly different. They were strangers in a strange land, empowered by their beloved prince to be ambassadors of the true king to their friends and neighbors.

This they sought to do with their whole hearts, and they resolved to continue living by the principles of the kingdom until the whole land knew the truth about their rightful ruler. It was not always easy, for they had come to understand how tirelessly their great enemy worked to divert their attention. They had become wary of his constant attempts to make them forget about their true kingdom and look instead to the supposed benefits of his reign. They fought these attempts with every fiber of their being, and though there were setbacks, the kingdom people remained faithful.

They lived as kingdom people until one day, suddenly, they did indeed hear a mighty sound in the distance. They looked as one to the edge of the sky and a great cry rose among them. They saw the regal banners appear in the distance …

talents, talents, talents

Imagine you've gone to the store to pick up a simple item—a package of batteries, a roll of paper towels, maybe some flour or sugar—just one thing. After searching through aisles and aisles in the enormous store, you finally find that one thing for which you have been looking. Then you begin the trek back to the front where the cash registers are located only to find that, much to your dismay, no fewer than 20 people are standing in line at every single register.

Even the supposed "10 items or less" lines are full, and most people in them have many more than 10 items. So you settle in, with your one paltry purchase, to wait. And wait. And wait.

Have you ever been in a situation like that? What is your general attitude toward waiting?

For you, what is the worst part about waiting?

In such a situation, you find yourself in the middle. You're no longer shopping, but you can't yet get in your car to go home. It's a period of waiting, and most of the time, we just try to pass the time so we can get on with whatever we plan to do next.

Unfortunately, a tremendous amount of time in life is spent waiting. We wait for a new job, wait for a spouse, wait for some change in circumstance. Our temptation during those periods is to simply pass the time, trying to get to the next thing.

Many believers live like their entire lives are about nothing more than getting to the end. The Christian life begins when you become a believer, and it ends when you meet Jesus face-to-face. But there is a great deal of time in the middle. For many Christians, that is missing time. It's a missing middle. But in the subversive kingdom, the middle isn't just something to get through—it's meant to be a very busy time.

> Read Matthew 25:14-30. What questions do you have upon reading this parable?

> How would you summarize the point of this parable in one sentence?

> What emotion do you think Jesus wanted to inspire with this teaching?

This story is often called the parable of the talents, though this particular use of the word *talent* is one not typical in our time. The talent referred to here is a sum of money—about six thousand *denarii*, which was equivalent to about a day's wages. Scholars have tried, with varying degrees of success, to relate that to a modern amount we can more easily understand, but suffice it to say that it was substantial. However, the talents play a secondary role to the overall point of the story.

This parable is about the middle and how the middle relates to the kingdom of God.

Read the previous parable in Matthew 25:1-13. According to verse 1, what is the kingdom of heaven like?

How do you think this parable relates to the parable of the talents?

The parable of the virgins is meant to inspire a sense of urgency and immediacy in believers. Similarly, the parable of the talents reminds us that in the kingdom, the time in the middle isn't just for sitting around and waiting for heaven. There is a great amount of work to be done. Gospel seeds need to be sown. Great darkness needs to be pushed back. Multitudes of God's lost children—our brothers and sisters—suffer under the oppressive hand of an evil tyrant.

In this passage, the middle is found between verses 18-19. It's that time between when the master entrusted his slaves with talents and when he came back for a report of what had been done with those resources—what had been done in the middle.

That's the time in which we're living. Just like the parable, there is a Master who has entrusted His people with resources. There will be a day of accounting. In the meantime, the time in the middle, we have to choose whether we will bury those resources or make the most of them. Therein lies the responsibility of the steward.

With which of the slaves in this parable do you most closely relate? Why?

What is one thing you might do today to begin to make the most of your own middle?

DAY 2 God entrusts

The parable of the talents is about a master who entrusted his resources to a collection of his servants. Two of the servants used those resources to earn even more, but the final servant did not. Instead, "The man who had received one talent went off, dug a hole in the ground, and hid his master's money" (Matt. 25:18).

Verse 19 continues, "After a long time the master of those slaves came and settled accounts with them." We're living in the time between verses 18 and 19. In the most basic sense, this parable is about money. But it's also more than that. The focus here is properly using what God has entrusted to us.

Why is it important to recognize that these slaves were stewards rather than owners of the talents?

When you see yourself as a steward rather than an owner, how does it change the way you use your resources?

The fact that the slaves were entrusted with talents implies stewardship. The master didn't *give* them anything; when he returned, he exercised his ownership of the talents. The slaves were expected to give back the principle plus anything they had earned.

Haggai 2:8 puts it like this:

> " 'The silver and gold belong to Me'—this is the declaration of the LORD of Hosts."

God, as the owner of all, has entrusted us with certain things. When we meet Jesus, we want to say clearly to Him, "What You gave me I used for Your glory, Your kingdom, Your purpose. I used well what You gave me."

> **Read through the parable of the talents again in Matthew 25:14-30. What specifically was entrusted to each of the slaves?**
>
> 1.
>
> 2.
>
> 3.
>
> **The Scripture indicates that the slaves were entrusted with different amounts. What might that difference in amounts mean to us?**

God decides what each of us receives from Him. This is a difficult principle for many people because we tend to compare our own gifts, resources, and personalities to those around us. We are tempted to look at a given person and wonder why they were gifted with more intelligence, more physical prowess, more musical ability, or more financial resources than we have been gifted. Conversely, we are tempted to secretly enjoy the thought that we have more than others.

Do you have a tendency to compare yourself to other people? Why or why not?

How do you think doing so affects your spiritual life?

How do you think God feels about that spirit of comparison among His people? Why?

In the subversive kingdom, people must come to the place where they can truly and honestly thank God for how He has made them. This is not a "positive thinking" message in which people simply feel better about themselves. Instead, it is a recognition that God has a plan and purpose for each of our lives. Because we believe that, we embrace the way we have been individually made and gifted in order to live out God's plan. This transformation in our thinking is fundamental if we are going to be a subversive influence in an "I'm OK; you're OK" world.

Read Psalm 139. How might the truth of this psalm impact the level of comparison in your life?

Which verses about God's knowledge of you in this psalm are most meaningful to you? Why?

God created each of us in an intensely personal and intentional way, yet if we refuse to acknowledge and accept His wisdom and handiwork, we will find ourselves incapable of making our greatest impact for the kingdom. "I can't serve the Lord because I can't sing." "I can't teach." "I don't have the gifts to do this or that." Kingdom people simply cannot think like that. Even if I cannot sing in a choir or praise team or do not have the gift of teaching, that does not mean I can do nothing. We must stop asking, "How can I be like someone who's different?" and start asking, "How can I live out what God has for me with what God has given me?"

When we not only acknowledge God's sovereignty in designing and forming us and actually become thankful for how He made us, we can begin to take advantage of what we've been given—whether it's one, two, or five talents.

What specifically might keep you from being thankful for the way God has made you?

Are you stewarding your gifts the best way you know how?

DAY 3 God expects

The parable of the talents acknowledges that God gives resources to His people as He sees fit. The parable records that the talents were given according to the ability of each slave. In other words, the opportunity for stewardship was based on the ability each person had already demonstrated to the master. His selections were not random; they were in no way haphazard.

With each assignment came a related expectation. The master entrusted his money to his slaves. Their job was not to question how much or how little they had been given but to use what they have been given in order to further the master's business.

Likewise, our job in the middle is to further the agenda, kingdom, glory, and honor of God. He expects this stewardship of us.

Looking back at the parable of the talents, how do you feel about the way the master responded to his slaves?

Does his response make you uncomfortable? Why or why not?

Read 1 Peter 4:10. How does this verse relate to the expectations of the master in the parable?

This master returned to find that the first slave had taken what was entrusted to him and made it into even more. He responded positively in Matthew 25:21:

> "Well done, good and faithful slave! You were faithful over a few things; I will put you in charge of many things. Share your master's joy!"

We experience an extra measure of joy when we have been faithful to live a kingdom-centered agenda during our time in the middle. It's true that such an agenda might not mean better health. It might not mean greater wealth. In the eyes of the world, living such a life might not seem to have any advantage to it at all; it might even seem foolish. But then again, is this not the subversive kingdom? What would make anyone think our agenda would bear any resemblance to the world's?

The extra measure of joy that comes with generous sacrifice, servitude, and obedience is hidden to the eyes of a culture built on power, prestige, and accumulation. For the Christian, however, it's very, very real.

Can you think of a time when you have shared in the Master's joy? What was that time like?

Did you find the joy to be worth the sacrifice? Why or why not?

Why do we tend to settle for lesser joys offered by the world?

It's encouraging that the second servant, though not quite as gifted as the first, received the same commendation from the master. He was not unfairly faulted because he had less to begin with; rather, the master was well satisfied because of his second servant's faithfulness. That is the true measure of success in the middle.

How is it a different measure of success to think in terms of faithfulness rather than amount?

Is the master's response to the second servant encouraging to you? Why or why not?

158

When we view our talents, our resources, and even our lives as our own, we have very little motivation to make something out of what we've been given. Instead, we conform our aspirations to those of our culture. Comfort. Enjoyment. Pleasure.

But when we embrace the truth of the parable of the talents—that in the kingdom, we don't own anything, and because God is the owner, He expects us to make the most of what we've been given—we find ourselves unleashed to use our resources to do good, for the sake of the kingdom.

The true Master expects this of us. A day will come when each of us will have to give an account for our lives, based on those expectations.

Do you believe God expects something of you? Why or why not?

How does fully embracing that expectation change the way you live?

DAY 4 God evaluates

"'Master, I know you. You're a difficult man, reaping where you haven't sown and gathering where you haven't scattered seed. So I was afraid and went off and hid your talent in the ground. Look, you have what is yours.' But his master replied to him, 'You evil, lazy slave!' " (Matt. 25:24-26).

What is your immediate reaction to this part of the parable?

What emotion do you think Jesus was trying to inspire with this section?

Those are strong words, especially in a day where the highest aspiration of most Christians is to live a good, moral life. That in essence is what normal Christianity has become: saying a prayer, getting baptized, trying to be a good person, giving some money to the church, and occasionally helping out a program, waiting for death to take us to heaven. This is hardly the kingdom life a good and faithful slave leads.

What does it look like for a person to bury their God-given talent in the ground?

Do you think people do this intentionally or unintentionally? Why?

Jesus had harsh words for such a person. A time will come when God will evaluate what we have done. Judgment is real and inevitable, even though most of us don't think about it very much.

How much do you think about God's judgment? Why?

How do you think He wants you to feel about His judgment?

Read 1 John 4:17. How does this verse say we should respond to the reality of God's judgment?

But this is where the parable of the talents gets really interesting. Notice the huge difference in the way the first two slaves and the third one approached the work. Strikingly, we see in verse 15, that the first man "immediately" went and put the talents to work in order to earn. Then, "in the same way," (v. 17) the second slave immediately got busy with the gift he was given. But the third slaves? You can almost sense the apprehension in his actions.

What should I do? Where should I go? Should I invest this way or that? And then finally, in exasperation, he digs a hole and buries his master's gifts.

Time passes and the master returns, asking what has become of what he left. Look again at how the first two servants respond. Both of them contain a word that's dripping with importance:

"Look!"

Can't you almost hear their voices? It's excitement! They have had a tremendous time in using what the master gave them and are now so very excited to show him. There is something innocent about their response—it's the response of a child who has just done something that pleases their father.

Now scan over to the reaction of the third servant. No excitement there. Certainly no happiness. And we see that whereas the first two were motivated by love and joy, the third slave was ruled by fear. His response makes you wonder if he could possibly be talking about the same master that the first two so delighted in pleasing!

He was afraid, and because he was, he was reprimanded for all he ever did was dig a hole in the ground.

The great news of the gospel of the kingdom is not that we have to use what we've been given; it's that we get to use what we've been given. When we begin to grasp that, we can look to the end, when our Master returns, not with fear but with great anticipation. We can look forward to the day when Jesus comes back and we too can say with exuberance, "Look! Look! I didn't have much, but look what I did with that you gave me!"

Are you using your gifts to advance the kingdom until Jesus returns? How are you using your position and resources to advance the kingdom? How are you seeking to honor the Lord with your free time? Are you giving consistently to His work? Are you finding a way to share Christ with your neighbors? All these questions must be asked if we are to make the most of the middle and if we are going to really find the abundant life of kingdom service that Jesus promises.

Do any of these questions resonate strongly with you? Which ones?

What other specific question do you think the Holy Spirit might be asking you today with regard to how you are using your life?

There is work to be done in the middle. There are talents to be multiplied. And there is great joy to be had. May we live in such a way that we share in the Master's joy as He looks with love and pride on us and says, "Well done, My good and faithful slave."

DAY 5 embracing the subversive kingdom

It is fitting, in a sense, that Jesus was so fond of using parables to describe the dynamics of the kingdom of God. The subversive kingdom itself is a grand tale of kings and servants, of love and rebellion, of subversive kindness and grace that transforms a world from the inside out. It is a story of the relentless grace that demands total allegiance and promises abundant life to all those who give themselves fully to it.

The kingdom today is the same kingdom as that of old. Even with so many tumultuous things going on in the world, we can stand firm, knowing Jesus is still on His throne. God is still at work, carrying out His plan and agenda. The subversive kingdom is certain to prevail, and we have the opportunity to join Christ in establishing it on earth.

> **Think back over the past six sessions. What is one truth that you think will be the most important to you in moving forward?**

> **What are three ways you hope your life is different because of this study?**

> 1.

> 2.

> 3.

Over the course of His parables, Jesus vividly illustrated the cost of the kingdom. He's shown us the proper response to the kingdom. He's pointed out that there are weeds sowed in the kingdom. But the very fact that Jesus couched these truths in parables, rather than plainly explaining them, reinforces the fact that the kingdom of God is subversive. It's hidden. God's kingdom has been planted within the culture of the world. Like a tree growing in the middle of asphalt, it sprouts up in the most unexpected ways and places; its roots slowly, irresistibly pushing out through the pavement, breaking it into pieces, destroying it.

The subversive kingdom is an unshakable universal reality, one which will never be snuffed out or stopped. But we have a distinct choice before us.

> Read Matthew 7:21-23. Have you ever read this passage before? Does anything trouble you about it? If so, what?

> What principle do you think Jesus was trying to communicate?

This is a disturbing passage of Scripture that ought to leave us breathless— hearts pounding, minds racing. It's a very stern warning from the Son of God. Perhaps what is most troubling is the level of spiritual activity attributed to the ones being rejected. Here are people well-schooled in spirituality—driving out demons, prophesying in the name of Christ, and even performing miracles—and yet there is no place for them in the eternal kingdom. Jesus' response to them in verse 23 is an Old Testament quotation:

"Depart from Me, you lawbreakers!"

What do you think Jesus meant by that last phrase? In what sense are these people lawbreakers?

Despite their level of activity, these very religious people have failed to do the will of the Father. Second Corinthians 13:5 exhorts us to take such a teaching very seriously:

> "Test yourselves to see if you are in the faith. Examine yourselves. Or do you yourselves not recognize that Jesus Christ is in you?—unless you fail the test."

The way you test yourself for authentic faith is not recalling whether or not you have prayed a certain prayer. The test is whether you are actively living in the will of the Father. True believers—those who have been born again by the Spirit of God and been transformed by the gospel—will seek to do the will of the Father. It's not the doing that saves them, but if they have been saved by the power of the gospel, they will walk in the evidence of that transformation.

The ultimate test of authenticity is found in Matthew 7:21:

> "Only the one who does the will of My Father in heaven."

The will of the Father is that His kingdom come. That is both our invitation and our responsibility as citizens of the subversive kingdom. We must bring the kingdom to bear in every situation of our lives, day in and day out, as we walk with Jesus through the rest of our lives in this middle time.

Transformational Church

How is your church **really** doing?

Before you can get where you want to go, you have to know where you are. The *Transformational Church Assessment Tool* (TCAT) can help. This on-line assessment uses a graded scale to gauge the perceptions of your church members concerning each of the seven Transformational Church elements: missionary mentality, vibrant leadership, relational intentionality, prayerful dependence, worship, community, and mission.

No other church assessment offers this much breadth and depth. This powerful online tool can help you quickly determine where your church is strong now and areas that need development. And reports are updated in real time and are available throughout the survey process for your designated leaders to review at any time.

Learn more at www.lifeway.com/tc

LifeWay | Leadership